FEARLESS

*The Life and Times
of a True Northwoods Trapper*

BILL RUTHERFORD

WITH CHET DUMASK

Wasteland Press

www.wastelandpress.net
Shelbyville, KY USA

Fearless:
The Life and Times of a True Northwoods Trapper
by Bill Rutherford

First Printing – July 2020
ISBN: 978-1-68111-362-3

Printed in the U.S.A.

0   1   2   3   4

To my good friend, Chet Dumask, for selecting me to tell his story, and for having the faith in me that I would tell it correctly

TABLE OF CONTENTS

INTRODUCTION

Ever since my book "Winegar Reflections- Tales from Wisconsin's Northwoods" was published in 2016, people have asked me, again and again, "When are you going to write another book?" I had been reluctant to do another one because frankly, I didn't think I had it in me.

I did, however, provide one caveat. I told everyone that the only way I would write another book would be if I could write about the life story of Mr. Chet Dumask. Chet is a life-long resident of Winegar/Presque Isle, a man nationally recognized for his trapping skills, a true outdoorsman, and a man who was never afraid to do what needed to be done for himself, his family, and his community.

If you bought this book expecting it to be a "How-To" book about trapping, it is not. The myriad of information and experience that Chet has accumulated in his 93 years could never be condensed into these pages. While there are going to be quite a few trapping stories in this book, you are also going to get an in-depth look into how a boy, along with his brother and sister, raised by a single mother in a town that initially didn't want them to live there, did whatever it took to survive and thrive in the harsh environment of Wisconsin's Northwoods.

For those of you who are only familiar with Chet Dumask though the stories in Winegar Reflections, this book will allow you to get to know him and admire the many things he has accomplished in his life. And, for those of you lucky enough to have spent some time with Chet over the years, as I have, you will truly enjoy hearing, in his own words, the stories and tales from a lifetime spent in "Wisconsin's Last Wilderness."

So, if you are ready to travel with Chet and I back to Winegar, pull your chair up a little closer to that warm fireplace, get comfortable, and let's get started…

CHAPTER ONE

The UN-Welcome Wagon

"I had to try and do everything in secret. In secret, right here in this town."

The town of Winegar, Wisconsin, in the early 1930s, was well on its way to becoming somewhat of a shadow of its former self.

Named Fosterville in 1905, when a lumberman named J.J. Foster opened a logging mill there, it eventually became one of the most successful logging towns in northern Wisconsin.

Mr. Foster, though, was not a good businessman, and the mill almost failed. In 1910, the Vilas County Lumber

Company, which owned the operation there, brought in a man from Grand Rapids, Michigan, named William S. "Big Bill" Winegar. Mr. Winegar and his father were significant investors in the company. He was responsible for getting the mill back on its feet, and the town now became Winegar, Wisconsin, a name that remained until it was once again changed, in 1955, to its present name, of Presque Isle.

During, and after WWI, Winegar was a lumber boomtown. When the logging operations were at their peak, the town boasted a population of almost 2,000 residents, nearly all of them tied, in one way or the other, to the Vilas County Lumber Company, and the mill.

In 1926, and in failing health, "Big Bill" Winegar sold the mill operation to William Bonifas and returned to Grand Rapids, where he died just a year later.

The logging operation in Winegar might still have been successful for many years, except for one fatal flaw. Apparently feeling that there was no end to the vast forests in the area, neither Foster, Winegar, or Bonifas, ever practiced what is now known as "reforestation," or the replanting of trees in areas where they had been harvested. Because of this monumental mistake, the heyday of the lumber industry in Winegar was about to end....

It was during those waning days of the now failing logging boom, that Ray Dumask arrived in Winegar, from Crandon, WI, looking for work. With him were his wife, Manda, and his three young children, Lambert, Violet, and Chester (Chet). A carriage worker by trade, Ray was unable to find suitable work that required his skills and he ended up working at the mill to support his family.

A few short years later, knowing the end of the mill, along with the jobs that went with it, was rapidly approaching, Ray was forced to go on the road to look for work, leaving his wife Manda in charge of the home, and the children.

The townspeople, mostly Finns, and Norwegians, had migrated to the area from Kentucky, and were engaged in one of the two main business' in Winegar- those business' being logging and moonshine. There were almost as many moonshine stills set up in the woods surrounding Winegar as there were logging camps, and trade with the lumberjacks and mill workers was very good indeed.

By 1935, the trees had been depleted, and the mill was moved from Winegar to Lake Linden, MI. The town was devastated. Most of the houses now stood empty, and almost every family in town was receiving government assistance.

As difficult as it was for the rest of the town, it was even more harsh for the Dumask family. Being of Polish descent, they were shunned by most of the people left in Winegar.

Chet tells us:

When we moved here, we weren't welcomed by some of the families in town because a lot of them were Finns and Norwegians, and we were Polish. A lot of them were "Kentucks," and that was where all the fightin' got started. Most of the problems were with the Spencer, Prosser, Peterlick, and Boring families.

When my mother would walk up the street to get groceries, the Prossers and the Peterlicks, and some others, would come out and throw old shoes and things at her and call her all kinds of filthy names. But she was a tough person. The women knew that they couldn't lick my mom. They were also jealous of her, because a lot of the men in town liked her a lot better than those other women, and they couldn't handle that. And mom got along well with the men too.

Not only was it a rough time for his mother, but Chet also had problems with the sons of some of those same families.

Ol' Tommy LaDean; he was about my mother's age. He was going around with one of the Prosser's. But he also liked me because, even though I was just a kid, I was a trapper, and he was also a trapper. He lived in Mercer, on Pardee Lake. He had a beautiful cabin there. And I heard from different people that his cabin was cleaner than any house in town. That's the way he lived, you see.

The Prossers, Peterlicks, Spencers, and the Boring boys were the ones who were always after me. They were about my age and size, but there were five of them and only one of me. And they would sic the Boring kid, Larry, on me, because he was the biggest one. But he wasn't real smart, ya' know. He was just big and dumb, let's put it that way. Yeah, they were quite the gang. I could run fast, but I still had to try and do everything in secret. In secret, right here in this town.

Of course, when I would come down the street, and I had some groceries, they would all come out and gang up on me. But, if I could get up to the Red & White store (at the top of Main St), and get the groceries without them knowing about it, then I was OK.

One day when I was about ten years old., Tommy LaDean was sitting on the bench down there by Mae Prosser's house. That was when they came out and grabbed my bike. He saw them boys ganging up on me, and he stepped in and stopped the fighting. He said to Dale Prosser, "Dale, you got boxing gloves. Go into the house and get 'em." Dale came back with the gloves, and Tommy said to the rest of the boys, "You kids make a boxing ring here. Drive some sticks in the ground and run some of that rope around them and make a ring. So, they did that, and then I had to box every damn one of them! The first one I had to fight was Dale Prosser. He thought he was a real tough boy, but I showed him that he wasn't tough at all. He was too slow to land any shots on me. I gave him a couple of good shots, and down he went. He was on his hands and knees, and he looked up at me and said, "I quit!". After that, I fought the next ones and whipped their asses too. The last one to challenge me was big Larry Boring. He was a lot bigger than me but had two strikes against him. He was slow, and he was stupid. I punched the hell out of him! I really hit him. I just kept on hittin' him; I wouldn't stop! Finally, he gave up and said, "I quit!", just like Dale had. I had to fight all of them before I could go home, and I whipped all their asses! When I was done and stepped out of the ring, Tommy motioned me over to him and said, "I knew you could do it!"

But that wasn't the end of it. We still had to fight the son of bitches after that. One time, Lambert and I were down by the railroad grade that ran between the two ponds, over by the big dam. Those boys were after us again. There were three or four of them, and they would gang up on us. Two of them would grab *you and hold you, and the other guy would be in front of you, punching the hell out of ya'. No way was I going to put up with that! I would have to hit a guy, then run, and stop and hit another one, and then run some more. Lambert was a good fighter too, and he could really hit. Anyway, a man named Matt Paschke saw us and came down there, and that put a stop to that fight right then! He told me, "If you need any help, you let me know."*

These incidents became a turning point and a milestone in Chet's life and most likely significant building blocks in molding him into the man he would become. You see, after he whipped all five of those boys, he was no longer afraid of them. Even though they still tried to fight him after that, they never would fight him one on one. They would always gang up on him if they saw he was alone. And Chet has never backed down from a fight the rest of his life, as you will see in future chapters.

(Larry Boring died in 1941 from complications of pneumonia. He was just 14 years old)

Later, I got a bike, and I had my dog, Duke, carry the groceries. So, we would be coming down the hill, and the Peterlick's dog, Bowser, would come bounding out of the yard, and go after him. So, this one time, when ol' Bowser came a-

runnin', Duke dropped the groceries and when Bowser got to the road, Duke just nailed him. He tore the livin' shit out of him! Let me tell you; that was the last time Bowser came out of the yard after my dog! Yeah, he learned his lesson that day, from Duke.

The Dumask family's struggles weren't just limited to the name-calling and the bullying. There was also a plan to restrict their weekly grocery allotment....

After the mill pulled out, almost everyone in town was getting government benefits. We, however, were getting shorted each week, because the town didn't like us.

The welfare truck came to town one day a week, and they would stop at all the houses. Well, all the kids in town would follow that truck around. And the truck would stop at everyone's house but ours. They wouldn't give us anything. The boxes had names on them, and the truck would come around, and the guy would take the box to each house. There was food in the boxes- a lot of cornmeal and stuff like that. Oatmeal, Flour, etc.... Other families were getting a beautiful hunk of roast in their boxes, but we couldn't get anything like that, for a long time. We had to go after them to try and get some meat and groceries.

That's when Roy Sipps, who was friends with my mother, stopped at the house one day, but he didn't see me, as I was outside somewhere. I heard him ask my mother,

"Where's Chet?"

"I don't know, "she replied, "but I am sure he is around here, someplace. What do you want him for?"

"I want to take him to Eagle River with me."

"What for?"

Roy said, "I want to show him to Judge Carter."

I came into the house, and Roy grabbed me by the hand and said,

"C'mon son. We're going to see the judge" Roy put me in his old Chevy, and off we went. You know, in those days to get to Eagle River (about 50 miles east of Winegar) was an all-day trip.

When we got to Eagle River, we marched right into the courtroom. Roy told Judge Carter who I was and what was going on back in Winegar. Now, Judge Carter and everyone around there was pretty much afraid of Roy. You see, Roy was in his court every few weeks, mostly for shooting deer. Roy said, "There has got to be a box of groceries on that truck for this kid and his family next week. Or you are going to hear from me!"

The Judge said, "But those people don't want his family in town."

Roy stood tall and looked Judge Carter in the eye.

"You heard what I said! There better be a box of groceries on that welfare truck for this family next week. Or you're going to hear from me!"

And the next week, and all the weeks after that, there was a full box on the truck, with the name "DUMASK" written on it....

CHAPTER TWO

Happy Mother's Day

"No matter how bad we had it, she didn't want to make things worse for anyone else. That was just the way she was."

The 1930s were not kind to the United States overall, and especially to the small northern Wisconsin town of Winegar. October 29th, 1929, a day known as "Black Tuesday", when the stock market crashed, triggered a worldwide economic collapse that lasted, for some countries, until the start of the second world war. This dark period became known as the "Great Depression", and it was the longest, deepest, and most widespread depression of the 20th century. Facing plummeting demand with few alternative sources of jobs, areas dependent on <u>industries</u> such as mining and logging suffered the most. The unemployment rate in the U.S. rose to 25%, and the rate in Winegar far exceeded that figure.

As noted previously, Winegar was already experiencing economic strife before the crash. Because the lumber barons had not practiced re-forestation, the area around the town was rapidly running out of available trees to harvest. Plans were underway to move the town's main industry, and in reality, the main reason for its' existence, the Vilas County Lumber Company, to Lake Linden, Michigan. The mill left town for good (or bad, as it turned out) in 1935.

When the mill moved away, so did most of the town's residents. There were many, many empty houses in Winegar, and almost the entire town was getting some form of government assistance. The future looked bleak for the tiny village.

Chet's father, Ray, was one of those who were forced to leave town to look for work, leaving his wife Manda, and their three children behind. While many of the townspeople banded together and helped each other out, that spirit of neighborly assistance did not extend to the Dumask family. They had to work and struggle for everything they got. Manda found what little work she could, and the boys, especially Chet, did what they could to help keep food on the table, and clothes on their backs. I believe that the strength and fierce determination to survive, that Manda had, she passed on and instilled in Chet, those same traits. He has never forgotten them, and that strength and determination have kept him going, without ever giving up, throughout his entire life. Let's let Chet tell us the story of this amazing woman....

During the summer, Lambert would go stay with my grandmother in Stevens Point and my sister, Violet, stayed with Chick and Donna Spencer, and I was the only one home. I was just a young kid when that happened. There was a guy there who wanted me to go and live with him and his wife in Chicago, and they would send me to school there. At that time, I kind of stuttered more. And both of them were concerned over that. But my mother would not let me go. So, they took Gene Tice with them, instead. Because my mom worked so much, I was left home by myself a lot. I sometimes took full advantage of that.

She had one of those stone crocks filled with homemade wine. We always got a bunch of dried fruit and stuff from where she worked. And that is what she made the wine out of. Once, while she was at work, me and Blake Phillips, we drank up all that wine. Strangely enough, we didn't get drunk, or even sick. That was some pretty good wine. Boy, she gave me hell for that!

Making Ends Meet

Mom was a pastry cook and she worked at Bay View Lodge for a while, and I helped out there also. I, along with another guy there about the same age as I was, took care of the boats and motors and things. Of course, when we had them all running then we would race them around the island in Presque Isle Lake. We especially liked going under the bridge there. Early on, you could go under that bridge wide open with a 5 ½ hp motor, and that sure was a lot of fun.

Then later she worked at Camp McKinley, over by Dairyman's Country Club, on Big Crooked Lake. She got the work over there through a guy that she knew who was a guide, named 'Swannee' Swanson. She worked there as a pastry cook, just like she did at Bay View Lodge. She worked, and she worked hard. And all these other women in town who didn't work were jealous of her. I worked there with her sometimes as well.

And that is how she supported us. I did things to help the family too. At that time I was catching a lot of mud minnows and I had to walk all over. I would walk down the railroad grade all the way out past the cemetery to where I had the traps. That was the shortest way. And my mom gave me this big hat to wear because of the sun. Those were some long, hot walks in the summer.

And then afterward there was a woman there, named Ruth Schneider. She would come up to Bay View Lodge with a guy named Walt. I think she was his girlfriend, because Walt's wife didn't like it up here, so he brought Ruth with him instead.

One day she was at Gunnar's bar. Of course, she knew that I was catching mud minnows and that I had to walk everywhere. She knew I was saving my money to buy a bike. She asked me," I understand you're saving your money for a bike.' I said, "Yeah, I am."

"How much money do you have now?"

"I think I have right around $12."

She said, "You bring me your money and I'll bring you a bike!"

I went home and got the money and gave it to her and on her next trip up here she brought me a really nice bike! So, now I didn't have to walk to get the minnows anymore That bike had a rack on the back, and I put two of those big coffee cans in there, with some netting over the top, so the minnows wouldn't splash out. Of course, one problem was that I had to really watch for the cars, Those sons of bitches, when they saw a bike on the road they liked to drive toward you and run you off the road. They came pretty close to me sometimes and the bike had these big 'buckhorn' handlebars, which would stick out pretty far, so I had to really be careful when there were cars were around.

When I was about 9-10 years old, I sold minnows off the front porch of our house. If I wasn't there, then my mom would sell them for me. That was before she started working at being a pastry cook, so she was at home a lot. There was one time that three guys come up to buy some mud minnows. I was home, and they said they wanted a couple of dozen or so. I counted out the minnows for them and they gave me a twenty-dollar bill. I had to go into the house to get the change, and come out and gave it to them. But, what I didn't know was that, while I was in the house, those bastards took all the rest of the minnows! Every minnow that was in the big crock was gone. They were in their car, going down the road, and I went to the crock to get ready for the next sale. I looked and there wasn't one minnow left there! They took the whole damn bunch. I never saw them again.

When I was 14 years old, I wanted to get a .22 caliber Springfield rifle from the Montgomery Wards catalog. (yes, folks, back then you could buy a rifle out of a catalog, no questions asked), *but Mom wouldn't let me. She said I was too young. At that time, you had to be sixteen to have a gun.*

My mother used to have this radio with a big battery, but she didn't have the money to buy the batteries for it. And we finally got electricity in our house. The house had been wired for electricity, but we never had enough money to get it turned on. So, we just had a lamp there. So, when we finally had enough money to get the electricity turned on, mom wanted to buy this little radio. So, she wanted the radio, and I had my heart set on getting this .22 rifle. It just so happened that the rifle was $7.50 and so was the radio. And I had $15.00. So, I made her a deal. If she let me have the gun, I would buy her the radio. I got it from the Montgomery Ward catalog. I gave her the radio and she was very happy about it. (Later on, I gave that rifle to my son, Mark. He said he wanted my first gun, and I couldn't think of a better guy to give it to!)

I used to have that radio here with me, but somehow it disappeared from my mother's garage. I know who took it, but I won't mention who it was.

The resorts weren't open in the winter back then. After deer season they pretty much shut down until Spring, Of course, that was long before the snowmobiles came about. Now the resorts that are still left here are open all year round.

In the winter I had saved up my money and bought a sled and I would haul water to different people in town. I would put a boiler on the sled and haul water from the little dam. I would haul that water and get 25 cents a barrel from them. One time I caught Vera Fairfield putting water into containers in the back part of the house. She had all the kettles and stuff filled with water she would take out of the barrel. I kept filling the barrel, but I was getting cheated on that deal. I didn't say anything to her, but I told my mother about it. She said, "Chet, don't say nothing. Those people don't have any money."

That was just the way she was. No matter how bad we had it, she didn't want to make things worse for anyone else. She never dealt with those women in town who were always giving her grief.

Gunnar Larson had the bar on Main Street. It was the Winegar Tavern, but everyone just called it Gunnar's. We lived just down the street in a big white house. (it is now the site of the Antique store). I don't know exactly how she and Gunnar got started. But I guess it was that she started as a cleaning woman for him, and after a while, she started tending bar there. Then Gunnar bought a bar on Highway W, across from where the Legion Post is, and my mother ran that for him. After the war, I used to spend a lot of time there with her. But after a bit, she didn't want to run that bar anymore, so Gunnar sold it to John McGee, and he ran it for some time. My mother came up to the bar in town then and worked there. Her and Gunnar became close and people in town thought of them as a 'couple', sort of like Frank Barta and Nancy Forslund down at the Standard Oil station.

Later on, we lived in that house kitty-corner from the bar. It used to be up on the second street, but my mom talked Axel Hill into moving it down where it still stands today. When it was still up on the other street we lived there during WWII.

Gunnar eventually sold the bar to Clyde and Laverne Alho. He then stayed across the street at my mother's house, and then they went to live in Arizona. That is where he passed away in 1976. I took care of getting him back up here and made the funeral arrangements for him. After the funeral, my mother and sister came up here for just a bit, then went back to their mobile home in Arizona, where they lived until my mom passed away in 1994. I brought her back up here and she is buried alongside of Gunnar.

I asked Chet if his mother was very strict with him, as a boy. He replied, *"I don't know about her being strict, but I know she was really proud of me bringing stuff home for us to eat. As I told you, when I came home with those two rabbits that I caught with the piano wire snare, she put her arms around me and she cried.*

CHAPTER THREE

It's A Trap!

"I blind set so much even other trappers couldn't find my sets."

Becoming a successful trapper is undoubtedly no easy task, nor is it an easy life. Traps must be checked daily, even in the harshest weather conditions. Heavy snow, howling winds, and temperatures that frequently plunge far below zero offer no excuse not to check your trap line.

When I was just a kid, I learned how to set a muskrat trap from a guy named William "Scrappy" Peterlick.

I asked him to tell me how to trap a muskrat. He told me that I needed to chop a notch in a log and put the trap there.

You have to notch the log so that the trap sits flat and doesn't slide off. On each side of the notch, you nail a half an apple. That's all there was to it.

But basically, I learned to trap on my own. I didn't listen to other trappers because they wouldn't ever say too much around me.

After I learned how to catch muskrats, I told the guys, "Anyone can catch muskrats; how do I catch mink?" Old Scrappy told me, "I'll show you how to trap a mink." But the only thing I ever caught with Scrappy was red squirrels. We would set traps where we thought were the right spots for mink, but all we ever caught were those darn red squirrels. Finally, I just went on my own. A lot of times, when you're trapping muskrats, you will also catch some mink. You have to study how the trap was set that captured the mink, then set some more the same way. It was different from catching the (musk)rats with the apples. And even later with the muskrats, I went away from using the apples, and just used blind sets, because I learned their habits, and I got better at catching them. Also, it made it easier to trap since I didn't have to pack a bag of apples with me every time.

NOTE: Blind sets are traps that are set without any bait in them.

As I said, I studied the habits of what I was after and learned from my mistakes. I never listened to any of those so-called "expert" trappers, who really didn't know crap about it. I blind set so much that those other guys couldn't even find my sets. I mean nobody could find them! They were concealed as much from the humans as they were from the mink. One time, the game warden, Ben Bendrick, went out with another trapper from Boulder Junction, named Eddie Thrall, to try and find my traps and check the ten cent tags on them. Even with both of them looking, they couldn't find my sets. That's how well I hid them.

You always have to conceal the trap from the mink. I even set like that for muskrats, even though you don't have to hide them as much. But I always do. It is just in me to protect all of my traps like that. I was hiding the traps just as much from the humans as I was from the animals.

One time, Bill Conway set his trap right on top of mine, and he never even saw the one I had already set, because it was so well hidden.

I had a set for mink, in between the two Horsehead Lakes, in the water. Of course, I camouflaged it nicely, so that neither you nor the animal could see it. Anyway, I went there to check the set (trap), and I looked, and said, "What the heck is that there? I went to move it, and I looked and saw that it wasn't even my trap. I said, "I bet that trap is Bill Conway's." Sure enough, he set his trap right on top of mine, and never sprung my trap! We were great friends, and he was a tough boy who used to help me in a lot of fights. He was bigger than me, and when the others would start to gang up on me, he would jump in and help me. I went over to his house, and I told him about the trap he set on top of mine. He laughed and laughed. I said, "I never moved it; you can see exactly how it is." Then he went out and picked up his trap.

A lot of the other trappers would run my line to see where and how I trapped, so they can learn from me, even though I was a lot younger than most of them at the time. The only thing that was ever told to me was how to set that first trap on that log, with the apples, to catch muskrats. Everything else about trapping, I taught myself.

First mink set

The first setup I had for catching mink was actually one of my 'rat sets. There was high water there and a big blowdown from a cedar tree. The water was right up to the log, so I put a #1.5 trap there. You only use a number 1 or 2 trap for mink, you know.

Anyway, I caught my first mink when I was trapping muskrats down in that marshy area over there by Little Horsehead, at the end of the railroad tracks, near the culverts. I was about fourteen years old, and I trapped a lot of 'rats. In the winter back then, there were a lot of muskrat houses, and we were allowed to set traps on them if we wanted to.

I watched the mink and learned about their habits. I told Billy Kunschke how to do it. We were good friends in grade school, and he was with me, in the boat, on Oxbow Lake. So, I told him, "I want to set a couple of mink sets out here." And Billy said, "Ya, that's ok."

So, we went just off where the Kunschke's lived and went by that big island. Maude Canfield owned that island back then. We went around there, and I found an excellent spot to set a trap. I said to Billy, "Let's go there! We can catch a mink there!" And we did! Billy was pretty impressed!

When you had to live in the kind of depression that we had, you have to do something. My brother, Lambert, didn't help much, especially with the trappin' I was doing. He only followed me that one time, because my mother kicked him out of the house, and that was the time he saw Russell May springin' my traps. Matt Anderson had given Lambert and me each a dozen traps, but Lambert didn't use his, so I took them and set them myself.

Matt Anderson was quite a drinker, and he came into Gunnar's a lot. That is where he learned that I was a trapper. And Tommy LaDean knew I was a trapper too.

NOTE: You may recall the name, Matt Anderson, from "Winegar Reflections. He and Alix Garas were sharing a cabin in the woods outside of town. In 1958, while both of them were drunk, they got into an argument. Matt Anderson ended up shooting and killing Garas. He left Garas' body lay for a few days until he sobered up and made it into town to report the incident.

I was trapping in a marshy area one time, and a kid about my age, Russell May, was messing me up. I would go thru and set my traps, and he would come along behind me and spring them. And, my brother, Lambert, caught him doin' it. My mother had sent Lambert outside one day, and he was following me when he found Russell springin' my traps.

Russell was the kid I was with when those game wardens caught us with some walleye down by the river. We had about three walleyes when the game warden, who was a big S.O.B from Mercer, named Swanson, came by and told us to get out of there and that he didn't want to see us there again. Swanson would pick on us, but strangely enough, he never pinched any of those Michigan guys. I think he was afraid of them because those guys would gang up on you. Anyway, Russell was pretty scared and said "Hey Chet, will you go home with me?", And I said I would, so we went up to the path along Little Horsehead there, and when we got to his house, Russell went in there and he went up to his mother and clutched her apron. He looked up at her and said: "Ma, I shit my pants, but I'll clean 'em!"

As a kid, I was only trapping mink and muskrats. I am a 100% mink trapper, always have been. I used to trap 80-85 mink a season. In two weeks! One year I caught 112 mink! And, I will tell you that if you can catch that many mink in a couple of weeks, then you sure as hell know how to trap! Because when you water-set, you only got two weeks, and then, you know, you are iced out. So, you have to give 'er hell the first two weeks. And that's where it counts, so I was pretty busy for those two weeks!

I learned by watching the mink and studying them. When we would get light snow, I would put out bind sets (no bait). That way, you don't, except on rare occasions, catch a raccoon or something. If you do catch a 'coon, they will tear up the damn place, and then it ain't suitable for mink trapping. Because, if a mink comes up and sees that, he is either going to hit the water or the high land, to avoid that mess.

We never had raccoons around in those days. We didn't have any raccoons around until many years later. When the 'coons came in, they just screwed everything up.

The Piano Wire Caper

When I was first getting into trapping, I was talking to ol' Scrappy Peterlick about trapping rabbits, and he told me that piano wire makes a real good wire for snares. You can use it for that because it doesn't kink. And that's all he told me about it. But, in my head, everything was always turnin', learnin', and rememberin'.

I wanted to catch some rabbits for my mom, but I didn't have any wire to make a snare. The wire that was mostly used for snares was some braided wire, but there was none around.

All the old guys in town had bought it all up, and now there was none available. But wait! I remembered what Scrappy had told me earlier. I knew where there was some snare wire, and I knew how to get it. So, over that next weekend, I snuck into the school and cut off a hunk of wire from Mrs. Larsen's piano. I cut off enough to make two snares.

I set up the snares out by Tug Spencer's farm. He had a big field there, and a fence. There were two holes in the fence, and I knew that the rabbits would run along that fence until they came to those holes, and then they would dart through them and go. I set the snares there, and I caught two rabbits. I walked into the house with those two rabbits, and when my mother saw me, she put her arms around me, and she cried. That was the only food we had.

I went back to school on Monday, and we gathered around the piano just like we always did, and Mrs. Larsen started to playin'. She is playing along, and she would hit a particular key, and it would just go "THUNK." She kept playin' and got another "THUNK" in the same place, you know. I thought to myself, "She knows!" Then I got to thinkin' about it some more, and I thought, "I bet my mother told her since mom knew I had taken the wire. And she probably had told her ahead of time already, just to cover up for me. She must have done that to let Mrs. Larson see that I stole the wire to catch some rabbits because we needed the food. So, when Helen (Mrs. Larson), got through the second time, she looked right straight at me and smiled. I knew then that she knew. Somehow she must have gotten some more wire later and got the piano fixed because I never heard a word about it again.

Trapping Minnows

As a kid, when I wasn't in school or helping my mom at work, I worked hard at learning how to trap. Another thing I caught was minnows; mud minnows mostly. I started doing that when I was only about 6-7 years old, and I sold them off our front porch. I don't really remember how I learned it, but it was just basic trial and error again. Anybody can trap minnows (this author can't!). *It is pretty simple. You just look at a minnow trap, and you will know what to do with it. I knew where to set it and how to set it. And I learned more by my mistakes. I learned that you must set it just right or it won't work. Again, it was all about trial and error. You learn the habits of what you are trapping by watching. You want to catch chub minnows* (chub and mud are small minnows, 2-4 inches in length), *you need to watch them, and learn their habits. I learned by my mistakes and by watching the minnows, and after a while, I got really good at catching them.*

*Same way with trapping mink. I learned from my mistakes.
This,* (tapping his head) *remembers mistakes. I got good at it
that way. And I got better than some of the adults.*

*But you know, when you are a good trapper, you catch stuff,
and these other guys were always playing around with the sets. I
had this one excellent spot right next to this little river, north of
Presque Isle. I knew that was an excellent mink spot, so I put a
set there. Just a blind set with no bait or nothing. But that was
the way I trapped mink. I never baited mink traps. Mink will
kill their own food. They like fresh food. Once you learn that
about them, you don't bait anything. Everybody but me baited
for them.*

*I wanted to widen my trap line, so I went down toward
Boulder Junction by Highway K, and I swear that you couldn't
stand it by the river, because of the stink. Everywhere you looked,
there was a damn muskrat carcass hangin' on a stick! A rotten
'rat carcass. I say to myself, "I'm out of here!" I mean, they would
drive every mink out of the country with that because they don't
know mink. The other trappers would hang carcass, after
carcass, after carcass. I got the hell out of there and never trapped
there at all. And I know they never caught any mink like that.
No mink is going to go after bait like that. Because again, mink
kill their own food. They like fresh food.*

I ran into one guy that came though from Mercer. And he "pocket sets' all the time, with bait.

Note: A pocket set is where you put a trap in a hole in the river bank.

He would only have it in there for a couple of days, and then he would take the carcass out and throw it in the river, and he would put a fresh one in the set. He knew that mink liked fresh meat. I knew what he was doing because about every three or four days, every little way, the was a rotten muskrat carcass out in the middle of the river, on the bottom. That's how I knew what he was doing. I would never do that. I walked by his truck once, and you couldn't stand the smell, from all those rotting muskrat carcasses in the back. But, as I said, I never baited my mink traps. And I caught the mink, and they didn't! Whenever you would get snow, I could see that the mink would avoid his sets. They would go around the set. They would either hit the water, or they would hit the land. So, I would use a blind set, because I knew where they were going and how they went. You have to understand that animal; you have to learn his lifestyle, which I did. I learned it on my own; I didn't have anybody tell me. I started trappin' muskrats, you know- just a punk kid, with a trap here, and a trap there. And I did it with that set I told you about, with carving a notch in the logs, and putting the trap there, and nailing half and apple on either side. And the 'rats would run that log, and I would catch them. And every once in a while, I would catch a mink!

I watched a mink one time. It was at the inlet of Mud Lake, where it empties into the Presque Isle River. I was on one side of the river. I jumped a mink, and he swam across the river, and he came up to this one log. It was a hollow log, and I had a trap in there. I decided to go across there to check that set. He went into the log, and I watched him, and then he went out of the other end. I waded across the river, and he saw me and ran back thru the log again without hittin' the trap. He had run across the trap in there twice, and never sprung it! Now that tells you something. That will get you scratchin' and thinkin'. You have to look at it like this- he can run through the log and miss the trap, so let's give him a little jumpin' pole. So, I put a stick in the log that he would have to jump over, and when he jumped, he would land right on the trap! The next time he went through there, I got him! You just have to think about things and use your head, and then you learn how to do something. Later on, I never set traps in hollow logs or tree stumps, but when I was just a kid startin' out, I was still learnin'.

I know that mink are real fast-footed. The foot is down, and it's up- just that quick. So I always set my traps real lean, with only a small amount of foot pressure to spring them, so that when they would just touch it, or just start to go into it, it would

33

spring. So you use a real light set on the pan, if the mink just barely touches that pan- BINGO! That's how you have to set them, and that is how you will catch the mink. I don't mind sharing that bit of info, because I don't trap mink anymore. I used to trap them when the pelts were sellin' for $20-$24, but when the price went way down to about $7, I would rather just let them go since it wasn't worth it. So, when it got down to $7, I just shut it down.

At this point, I mentioned to Chet that I had read in a trapper's book that they were setting traps to spring with three pounds of pan pressure, and his response was, *"What the hell were they trappin', a bear?"*)

But now that he has trapped these animals, what's next? Read on to find out…

CHAPTER FOUR

After the Catch

"It tasted pretty good. Yeah, it tasted just like a muskrat should taste."

Of course, a trapper's work is not finished with just catching the mink, muskrat, beaver, and other animals. As difficult as it is, especially for a boy, to run a trap line, even with just a few dozen traps, imagine what is needed to be done with the animals after he catches them. Well, you don't have to imagine it. Let's let Chet tell you what happens when you get the animals home....

I learned from Roy Sipps and Scrappy Peterlick how to skin the catch. Bob Eesley could skin a rat in about a minute. When he and I were out in the woods together, he would clean skin the beaver, and I would skin the muskrats.

When I would get back home, I would keep my boots on, and I would hold the muskrat between my knees, and I would skin it. I would pull the skin from the tail down. But I thought this method was a bunch of crap. So, I came up with a better plan. I put a nail through the tail of the rat and nailed it to the post by my minnow tank. Then I would start pulling the skin down. Later on, when I had the vise and a woodworking table, I would just put the tail in the vise. It was a different method from the way other guys skinned 'em, but it worked well for me. (This was another example of Chet's ability to see a problem, and then come up with his own method of solving that problem.)

Once you have the pelt, you nail it on a board to dry it out. I would mostly throw away the carcass, but sometimes I would save part of it to use for bait for other animals. Some of the old-timers would want the carcass. People would even eat them. Hell, I've eaten them. You take the hind legs and the front legs and a chunk out of the back and cook 'em up. It tasted pretty good. Yeah, it tasted just like a muskrat should taste. (Author's Note: I have absolutely no idea of how a muskrat "should" taste…) *They taste something like a rabbit since they both are vegetarians, so their diet is similar.*

Selling the hides

After the pelts are dried, then they are ready to be sold. Mink sold for a pretty fair price. They used to run just over $20 each. The muskrats varied in price, from $.50 up to $4.00, and then they would come back down.

A fur buyer would come into town. I used to sell my pelts right out of my house to him. Most of the time, he had a place that he would stop, and everybody would go there. Then you would have all the "gapers," and they would know exactly how much you caught and everything. They wouldn't leave there until the place locked up. I didn't like that set-up, so I told the fur buyer, "If you want my stuff, you are going to have to come to my house. No one else sold like that. I was the only one because, in reality, I was the only one who had anything to speak of. I was trapping and selling like that as a kid, and the buyers would come to the house, usually late at night. I would hear my mother tell 'em, "Well, he's sleeping. I'm not going to wake him up." I would yell, "Mom! I'm awake!" She would let them come in, and we would sell the stuff to them.

The trapping season was in winter, as they usually didn't let you go out until everything was frozen up. But it is hard to trap rats and mink when everything freezes up. And you couldn't trap on a 'rat house, so you had to stay the hell away from there. It was the darn DNR that kept putting all these roadblocks in our way.

Then, as time went on, the DNR would finally give us some open water trapping. I am sure it broke their hearts to do that. But, you know why they did it? It was all because of the school kids. When they had Christmas vacation, they could then go out and trap. So that is the reason. They were strict with us guys, but they gave in to the kids.

You had to be careful then. I remember the family that had the Shady Rest resort on Presque Isle Lake. The husband and the wife did not get along, and they let the kids run wild. The kids would steal your traps. I caught them once coming back up the river over here, in the canoe. I went down there with my snowmobile, and they heard that. Then they dumped the traps out of the canoe, but I saw them do it. I said, "You go down there and pick that stuff up that you threw in the damn creek!" But they wouldn't do that, so I told them, "Well, I'll go pick them up, and then I'll have somebody come over and knock on your door." And I did. Their mother, you know, she had a hell of a time with those kids. It wasn't all one family; it was two different families of those kids.

I had a hell of a time to get the wardens to handle it. One of the wardens liked that woman, you see. So, he let the kids off easy. But they never gave me any more trouble after that.

Chet did have some run-ins with a few of the wardens back then, from both sides of the state line. But that is for a later chapter of this book....

CHAPTER FIVE

Walkin' on the Fightin' Side...

"All of a sudden, he opens the door of his truck, and pulls out this huge shotgun!"

I believe that Chet always had the attitude that, if you left him alone, he would leave you alone. He was comfortable learning things on his own and he tried to never rely on others for help.

There are people in this world, however, who just can't leave others alone. Not only do they want to know your business, but they are also always trying to mess with your business.

Some of them think they are tough (especially when they are in a group of their friends), or they perceive others to be weak and are therefore susceptible to being bullied and picked on.

A number of these unfortunate bullies soon learned the hard way that Chet Dumask was no weakling, nor was he afraid of any of them. He never instigated a fight, but he never backed down from one either.

As we outlined in an earlier chapter, Chet, as a boy, fought and beat five other boys, one after another. Here are his accounts of some of the other fights he was involved in....

We used to go up to Wakefield a lot. I was going with a girl from Wakefield, and her brother was up there. I'm sittin' in the booth with this gal, and he keeps comin' around all the time, and saying, "Well, there ain't nothing to do around here on Saturday night except fight. But I just ignored him. He came back the second time and the third time, and he was sayin' the same thing....

Finally, I said to him, "Are you invitin' me to fight you? Is that why you are tellin' me all this?"

He says, "Yeah!" I told him, "Ok, I'm on!" So, we went out into the parking lot, and I just punched the livin' shit out of him!

And, of course, Earl Spencer was there and heard about that, and then he wanted to fight me as well.

I told him, "I am just a punk kid, and you're a full-grown man. But if you really want to fight, let's go." "C'mon," he says.

"But don't stop by the door!" I warned him. You see, his trick was once he got out the door, he would step to the side, and when you came out-WHAM! He said he wouldn't do that and out we went. He found out real quick that he had bumped into someone a lot tougher than he was. So I fought Earl, and I whipped his ass too. He was a heavily built, muscular guy, and he was about forty pounds heavier than me. But I punched the livin' shit out of him too that night. You would never have gotten any of the Spencer's to admit that I had whipped his ass. But after that, he never came after me again. He left me alone from then on.

Anyway, after I whipped his ass, I went into the men's room to wash the blood off my hands, and the first guy I had fought came in. He wanted to congratulate me! "That was a good fight!" he told me.

I said, "With you or with Spencer?"

"Both! I didn't think you could lick him."

"Well," told him. Guys like him might be tough, but they can still be beat".

That's how that works, I guess. They all want to fight you, but after you whip their asses, they don't want to ever fight you again....

My brother, Lambert, was a lot smaller than me, but he was a good fighter. He was a hell of a good fighter. We did a lot of fightin' in town. Whenever we were together, nobody messed with us. We would whip the shit out of everybody.

Swede Prosser was a good friend of mine, all the way through the service and even after we got back home. But Dale Prosser, he was different. Dale was an Earl Spencer type boy. And he thought he was tough. But in high school, my brother, Lambert, and I beat the shit out of him. And the cop stopped Lambert and Dale one day when they were fightin' down by Ted Christensen's grocery store. And the cop (Ofc. Schwartz) says, "Who started this?" Lambert pointed his finger at Dale, and Dale says, "I did." The cop says, "Ok. I'll remember that." And after that, Dale left my brother alone.

There was another girl I went with for a while. She wrote to me the whole time I was in the service, and we went together for a while after I came home. Then we got in a big fight at a bar in Hurley. I got into it with her uncle. I didn't know him at the time. She didn't want to go home with me because I was drunk. She wouldn't let me drive. So, she was going to stay there. That's when all the rig-a-ma-role got started. Swede Prosser was with me. Of course, he wasn't any help at all when it came to a fight.

So, anyway, I went outside, and the girl's uncle followed me out. Next door was another bar, but it was closed. There was a set of steps there. I went up those steps, turned around and said, "You want a piece of me, you're gonna have to come up here." He did! And boy, I gave it to him good.

I never really ever lost a fight when I grew up. Even with that game warden, Bowmaster. Oh, he thought he was tough, let me tell you. But he ran into somebody that kind of changed his mind about that. Me! (The incident involving, Warden Bowmaster and Chet is detailed in Chapter 11 of this book)

CHICK SPENCER FIGHT

Tug Spencer was Cora Spencer's husband, and he was a little screwy. He told Chick Spencer and all his buddies that I had been picking up all his traps. And then, one morning, Chick and his friend, Richie Nemo, were down at Riverside bar drinkin'. Somehow they got the idea in 'em to come up to the house and beat the shit outta me. So, Chick comes up to my house and stands outside, hollerin',

"C'mon out! C'mon out!" He yelled.

"What for?'

"C'mon out! I want to talk to you'."

"Yeah, ok."

I had just got out of bed, and I was only half-dressed. I stepped out, and I see this fist from Chick Spencer, coming at me!

I said, "What the hell is going on?"

Chick yelled, "You ain't going to cut the liver out of my old man and get away with it!"

Old Tug had gone and told them that I was going to cut his liver out, which I had never even said. So, I had to fight Chick about that. I kept telling him, "Knock it off, Chick! Knock it off!" Finally, the fight was over (I won, of course), and Chick said: "C'mon down to Riverside, and I'll buy you a drink."

"Ok" I went in and put the rest of my clothes on and went with him.

We got to Riverside, and Richie Nemo was waiting for us. He was surprised because he thought I was going to get the shit kicked out of me. Richie looked at me, and he looked at Chick, and Chick was all beat to hell. But that was the way those people were. By then, everyone knew I was not afraid of anyone, and that I could fight.

I was out sharpening my chain saw in my mother's garage one day, and some guys came by and shouted, "C'mon Chet! There are some guys in town that want to fight!"

"What guys?"

"Some guys from Marenisco."

"Ok! I'll be right there!'

By the time we got there, all the Marenisco boys had taken off, and we couldn't find them. I went over to Marenisco and looked all over hell, but I couldn't find them. I bet they took the backroads so I wouldn't catch up with them.

It was just a lot of envy and jealousy. And at that time, it was about trapping and stuff. You see, I could trap then, and I can still trap.

Almost shot by Carl Stephens

When I was in high school, there was one guy, Carl Stephens, and he almost shot me! I had traps set on the north end of Presque Isle Lake by a great big uprooted tree. It was a perfect spot! When I set traps, I always use a hidden stake, you see. I take the stake, and I drive it all the way down and cover it up. I came by one day, and there was a big branch stuck down in by my set. I pulled that son of a gun out, and there was a goldarn trap on it. And it ain't mine! It was Carl Stephens' trap. So, I stuck it in the roots of that downed tree and left it there. The next time I came back, it was set right there by my set again. He had picked up my trap and hung it up on a tree there. I walked the shoreline of Presque Isle Lake to check some other traps that I had set there. I came back out onto the road, and there, parked on the road, was Carl Stephens. He says to me, "I sprung your trap down there, and I am going to spring it every time you set it."

I told him, "Well, I am going to go down there right now and set it!"

Carl was in his vehicle, and we are talking back and forth, when all of a sudden, he opens his door and pulls out this huge shotgun!

When I saw that, I gave it a kick. I kicked it out of Carl's hand. But when it hit the road, it went off. BOOM!

When that happened, he was so sacred he damned near cried. I said, "You could have killed me, Carl. Is this worth it? You know I'm in the right, and you know I won't give up. So why don't you just leave me alone?

"Now, if you want to trap down there on the lakeshore, go down on the shore and trap. But don't ever set on my trap, or right next to it, again."

"Ya, ya, ok, Chet," Carl gave in. And after that, he left me alone.

He left me alone because I stood up to him. That was the way I was. He could have killed me right there. But of course, had I known that the shotgun was loaded, I may have acted a little different, mainly because I knew I damn goofy he was. He was a hothead, and every place I trapped, he was there. He would kind *of follow my sets. He looked a lot for my sets, you know. He never really knew how to catch a damn mink by himself.*

I told my mother about it later, and she said, "Don't say anything about it to people around town because they were always looking for trouble."

"Well, He was the one looking for trouble. He could have killed me." I told her. "What would you have said then?" She got a few tears, and she didn't say anything more. Mom was a good friend of Carl's wife, Vera, and they used to play cards together a lot. I guess my mother didn't want to upset Vera and get Carl in trouble at home.

CHAPTER SIX

Anchors Aweigh!

"I want you and everyone else to know. I wasn't drafted. I enlisted! My brother was drafted, but not me."

The United States passed its first peacetime draft, the Selective Training, and Service Act (STSA), in September 1940, and began drafting 21 to 35-year-old men in October of that year.

From that October, until the STSA was significantly reduced in 1947, the country drafted over 10,000,000 men. Of the 16,000,000 men who served during World War II, almost sixty-three percent of them entered military service via the draft.

But not everybody at that time waited to be drafted. Many men heeded the call of duty and enlisted in the various branches of the military. From large cities and small towns across the country, they came voluntarily, leaving behind wives and children, siblings, parents, friends, and relatives, to fight in the war, especially following the horrendous attack by the Japanese at Pearl Harbor, on December 7th, 1941.

As discussed elsewhere in this book, Chet was a fighter since he was a child. It was only natural then that, in 1944, even though he was only 17 years old, and had to lie about his age to the recruiter, Chet was able to enlist in the U.S. Navy, (his brother, Lambert having been drafted earlier). Chet had the option of a two-year enlistment, a four-year enlistment, or enlisting for the "duration of the war'. At that time, no one knew how long the war would last, and he could have been a sailor for a very long time. As it turned out, the war ended fifteen months later.

Camping with Lambert and Perry Doriot

I was a good swimmer, even when I lived here. I had people come out to Presque Isle lake, to watch me run off that dock at the resort by the Bay View Road there. People would come over there just to see me run and dive in. There was a guy named Rackner, who owned that resort at the time, and he used to get me to show off for those people when I was out there swimming with my friends. He had that beautiful long pier that we could run and dive in. It was about forty feet long, and we could really get a good run.

Just before Lambert left for the Navy, I took him and Perry Doriot camping out by Crab Lake. We camped on an island there. One of the women who lived there came over by us and was wondering who we were. But when she saw it was me, she said "Oh Chet! I didn't know it was you." Well, then it was OK. Otherwise, we would have gotten kicked off.

Later, I told Lambert, "C'mon. Let's go get some wood."

He said, "Well, there's some wood here."

"That ain't going to be enough. C'mon, jump in the canoe!"

We got in that canoe, and when I got us out a little ways from the island, I dumped the canoe over!

He yelled, "What did you do that for?" I said, "You're going in the Navy, Lambert. You better learn how to swim!" He wasn't the best swimmer in the world, you know. Of course, since it was a canoe, when I dumped it, I got soaked too!

Lambert later told me the story about how, when he got drafted, he was standing in line, and the guy at the table was asking the men, "Army or Navy?" Well, Lambert heard him doing this, and then the guy would tell them, "You can't have Navy." And he would stamp their paper 'Army.' And he got to

Lambert and said, "Army or Navy?" Lambert said, "NAVY." The man said, "You can't have 'NAVY', and raised his hand to stamp 'ARMY' on his paper. Lambert grabbed his hand and told him, "You asked me what I wanted, and I said NAVY!"

"OK! OK!" the guy said and stamped 'NAVY' on his paper. And that's how Lambert ended up in the Navy!

I had lied to the recruiter about my age. I was only seventeen at the time. As it turned out, they didn't call me until just after I turned eighteen anyway.

I started down in Illinois, at Great Lakes Naval Base, for basic training. When that was over, they sent a bunch of us out to the west coast. They sent us out there on a troop train, and that was not a good trip. We would go over those mountains, you know, and on the way down, you could hear those big steel wheels sliding on that track. It was kind of a scary ride, and it took a hell of a long time to get out there. We finally made it to San Francisco, but we were only there for a short time, as you will see.

I had wanted to go in for underwater demolition, and that is what I trained for, but then the war was over. I ended up only being in for 15 months.

We had just got started on that training, and the war ended. (and that is how I ended up on the USS Never Sailed)

I had done a couple of drop-offs, off the side of a PT boat. That is where they take you out and drop you off, and you have to swim over and stick something on the hull of a ship. Our training consisted of a lot of swimming, diving, and jumping. Sometimes we had to jump off the boat rather than dive. We had different heights we would jump from, the highest being 27 feet. From that height, you were supposed to jump in feet first. But a couple of times, I dived from there instead of jumping. That one time, I had to get pulled out of the pool. I had to lay down because I had hurt my back by diving from so high. I didn't tell them I had hurt my back because I knew I would catch hell since I wasn't supposed to dive from that height. Herb Doss, my friend from Ingram, WI, helped me out of the pool, and I laid there for a while until I got so I could walk. It had hurt pretty bad. You know you have to sometimes jackknife when you dive from that high. I had dived from that high before, but this time was just a really bad deal.

At the base in San Francisco, we had a motorcycle with a sidecar, and we used to pick up a lot of those prisoners. At that time, I was in the "Master at Arms" force, which was sort of like the Military Police. We were in this big building there. We would be picking up these guys and taking them where they had to go. These guys that were coming in would be on their way to the brig. There was one hell of a bunch of guys that were coming in from overseas. When they got to the base, we had to handle them. They were coming back, and we had to get them processed in and get *them some new clothes. We had a "lucky bag" there. It had all these clothes there that Herb Doss and I would give out to those guys. And, of course, I got my share of that clothing too.*

We had to take them from upstairs in that big building, load them on the motorcycle, and escort them to the brig. (These were guys that had done something illegal while they were overseas, and since the war was over, they were being brought back here to finish out their time here. But they were OK. They were good guys, you know. They just made a mistake somewhere along the line.

Some of them wanted to send a picture back to their girlfriends. We would even take a picture of them on the motorcycles. We also let them pose with a badge and an empty holster on them with the SP (Shore Patrol) guy. It was against the rules, but I figured, "Sure, why not? What the heck!" I didn't mind, but I knew the commanders sure would not have wanted me to do that. But I did it anyway, because, you know, if I were in their situation, I would want that too.

(NOTE: People in positions of authority never impressed Chet very much…)

A lot of the guys did some drinking in the Navy, especially when the war ended, but I didn't. I stayed away from that stuff. They would want to go to downtown San Francisco and get drunk, but I would mostly stay back on the base and out of that whole deal. I did go out with the guys sometimes, but I didn't drink with them.

When they announced that the war was over, you should have seen that town! People were really celebratin', you know! It was a big celebration, but it was pretty dangerous to be out and about at the time. It was just like a war, instead of the war being over. There was stuff coming out of the upstairs windows- bottle, chairs, everything. It was crazy!

I got tangled up with a good woman over there. And, of course, she wanted me real bad. I told her about where I lived, and all that kind of stuff. She was a bartender at one of the places we hung out. She was always way down to the end of the bar. I thought to myself, "I think I could get ahold of her!" And, of course, I did. She would go out the back way and then meet me out front and away we would go and have a good time someplace else. She had an apartment with another woman, and this other woman had a boyfriend too, so there would be both couples in this room. She wanted to come home with me. I told her what the situation was here because that was when my mother had this small bar over here that she was operating for Gunnar. Now, I knew how my mother was, how she was about women, and I knew if I came home with a woman, she definitely wasn't going to like it. So, I left that woman and went home. I told the guys, "If she asks about me, just tell her I said I'd be *back in a little while; that I had something to take care of. I just gave her a bunch of bullshit…. She was a good woman, though. I should have figured, "To hell with Mom, I don't care what she thinks. But I decided that since Mom wouldn't approve of her, I wouldn't do it.*

As I said, I had enlisted for the 'duration of the war,' and the war ended not long afterward, so they kicked us out. And wherever we got discharged from, we would get our travel pay from there (San Francisco) back home. But I and Herb, when we got our mustering out pay, which was around $600- $700, we hitched all the way home. (2000 miles). We made it to Chicago, and his girlfriend was there, and my girlfriend at the time lived in Sturgeon Bay. So, when we got to Chicago, we separated, and he stayed there, and I went north. Another friend of mine who went into the service was Bill Conway. Bill was a good man in the Army. He was a tough son of a bitch! He once killed seven Japanese in one bunch. His unit was in the brush, and he ran into these Japanese soldiers. Now, knowing Bill as I knew him, he would have been excellent in the woods. Real good with a rifle- a whole lot better than those Japanese. He ended up killing seven of 'em before the others ran off. The Army wanted to give him a big medal, but he refused it. Instead, they sent it home to his mother.

The last I knew of him, he had re-enlisted because, when he came back the first time, he had this yellow-jaundiced fever. It was so bad that it took both Lambert and me to hold him down when he would get that fever. Since he couldn't do anything out here, he went and re-enlisted in the service. He ended up in a hospital in Minnesota someplace. I had wanted to visit him, but he died before I could get there. He was probably around 23-24 at that time.

Only being in the Navy for fifteen months, you don't get to accomplish much. I did a hell of a lot of shooting there. You know, on that balloon that they would tow around. I could pop those off real easy. They always wanted me to come back and show the other guys how to shoot like that. Of course, I was always a good shot anyway.

CHAPTER SEVEN

Dangerous Waters

*"I did my part. I saved her life while
everyone else stood around doing nothing."*

Presque Isle is the home to over 70 lakes, which makes it an attractive vacation spot. Swimming, boating, fishing (both open water and ice fishing) are some of the area's main draws. But these same waters can also be places of danger if you are not careful, and respectful of the conditions.

In *Winegar Reflections*, we outlined some of the stories of people who have lost their lives in the waters surrounding the town. In this chapter, we will explore some of those tragic events in greater detail.

Chet was involved in the recovery of three bodies of people who had drowned, and he was responsible for saving the lives of two other individuals who certainly would have died if it weren't for him. In one of those events, he did have help from his brother, Lambert....

Both my brother and I had just completed artificial respiration training with Troop 62, our local Boy Scout troop. When we were going through that training, we never figured that we would actually use it, and we certainly never imagined that we would be using it so soon!

Lambert and I saved this girl, Alona Hieronymous, who couldn't make it back from the raft on Little Horsehead Lake. It was right down there by the point. There was a bench there, and that's how we got into the swimmin' hole. She was out at the raft there, and it had a diving board. She started swimming toward shore, and she got about halfway there, and, for some reason, she started dog paddling. Then she started gruntin' and moanin' and spittin'. She had already swallowed a lot of water, and she was going down. We jumped off the raft and swam as fast as we could to her. Lambert got to her first and grabbed her by the arm. I swam up on her other side and grabbed her. We both helped her get to shore.

There was a wooden platform there on the shoreline. We got Alona up there and laid her down. I held her head, sideways, so the water would come out, and my brother was giving her artificial respiration. She was spitting up a lot of water, but we saved her life that day.

The other person he saved was a woman who was fishing off the culverts that ran under County Highway B, by the Little Horsehead Lake boat landing. As you will see, Chet saved her life, but according to one person in attendance, he didn't do enough...

Part of the problem was that nobody else would do a damn thing! They all just stood around, yelling for someone like me to help out. When Mrs. Smith fell in Little Horsehead, there was a bunch of people there, but they would have let her drown if I hadn't done something.

She was fishing off those culverts there by the boat landing. She was wearing some heavy wool hunting clothes at the time. Well, she hooked a fish, and the damn thing pulled her off the culvert and into the water. She drifted down to the snag and grabbed a branch, and was hanging on for dear life.

I had my store on Main St. at the time, and somebody came running in to tell me what happened. I jumped in my jeep and drove out there. Her husband was standing up on the road by the guardrail post. He was jumping around and yelling for someone to help her. I went to him and asked, "Where is she?"

"Hanging on down there!" he said, pointing to where his wife was located. So, I went down there, and there were already some people there, Robbie Symanski was one of them that I remember.

I went out by the snag, and I asked her, "Are you OK?"

She said, "Yes, I'm OK."

"No broken bones?"

"No, I am just really tired," she said.

Those big cumbersome wool hunting clothes had helped keep her afloat at first, but when they got soaked, they were really heavy.

I told her, "Just grab onto me and hang on! If you can't hang on, let me know." She grabbed me and hung on, and I had to swim up a little way before I could touch the bottom. I finally was able to touch, and then I could help her. I got almost up to shore, but the water was still pretty deep. Robbie Symanski was there, and I yelled, "Give me a hand here!"

He waded out and helped me get her up and out of the water. By that time, the ambulance was there. Big John Eschenbauch was there, you know, and they put her in the ambulance and took her to the hospital.

Holy shit! The next day, they were saying, "Dumask never even took the water out of her!" I did my part. I saved her life while everyone else stood around doing nothing. The ambulance guys took her as soon as I got her out of the water, so that was the end of it for me.

But the next day, her husband came into the store. He started complaining because I hadn't gotten her fishing pole out of the lake when I was in there! A damn bamboo pole that probably didn't cost more than a dollar, and he was pissed that I didn't save that, along with saving his wife.

I was tempted to light into him, but I figured, "What the hell can you say to people like that?" I should have said," You are f-ing nuts! Why in the hell didn't you jump in and pull her out? She's your wife!"

But he was no different than the rest of them that were there. Just stand around and wait for someone else to jump in, and then bitch about it later. The more you do, the more you get ridiculed for doing it.

John Austen owned the Annabelle Lake Resort, about three miles west of Presque Isle. He was good friends with Chet, and Austen often paid Chet to chauffeur him around the county to various 'watering holes.' One evening, while driving his Cadillac back to the resort, Austen failed to negotiate the right-hand curve on Highway B, by the same boat landing where Chet had saved that woman before. His car left the road and ended up submerged in the lake, upside down. Chet can fill us in on what happened....

I used to tend bar at Gunnar's a lot back then, and John would come in and ask Gunnar if he could have me for the rest of the day. I would drive him to all the taverns around the area. I used to get $100 a day to drive him to drink. And then one day, I was in there tending bar, and John comes in there, and he starts laying out $100 bills on the bar -five of them. And then he pushed them over to me. I said, "What do you want to buy with that, John?"

He says, "Those are for you."

"Well, what for?"

"Because I like you, that's what for."

John had been drinking at Gunnar's one night and was heading home in his new Cadillac, to his resort on Annabelle Lake. He missed the curve by Little Horsehead and crashed through the guardrails and into the lake. His car ended up upside down.

By the time I got to the accident, there was already a whole bunch of guys in the water, but they couldn't get the door open. And here is why. The car was upside down, and they were trying to pull the door handle as if the vehicle was right side up.

Author's note: In those days a cars door handles stuck out a little from the side of the car, and to open the door you pushed the lever handle down.

They were pushing the door handle in the wrong direction and couldn't figure out why it wouldn't work. They were pushing the door handle DOWN when they should have been pulling it UP instead. I went down in the water and had no problem getting the door open other than the water pressure from inside. John's body was in the back seat. He was a pretty big guy, but I got him out of there and up onto the shore, but it was too late to save him.

Glenn Fairfield loved to fish, and his favorite fishing spot was just outside of a weed bed on Big Horsehead Lake. Chet happened to be out checking his trapline nearby when Vern Aiken came running to tell him that Glenn had fallen out of his boat, and he was afraid that he had drowned.

Glenn was out fishing by those rushes on Big Horsehead, and you can see the spot he was at, from Hwy B. I was out trapping muskrats, and when I was doing that, I always had my pram in the back of my jeep. I was driving down the road, and here comes Vern Aikens. He was wet all the way up. Vern apparently had tried wading out to help Glenn but could not get out there because the water was too deep. He says, "Glenn Fairfield drowned out there! He was hanging on to his boat, but he only has that one hand!" I grabbed my pram and put it in the water right there and rowed out there to where Vern said that Glenn went down. I found him, and he was in the same position as little Bobbie Lahaie was- face down on the bottom, arms and legs spread. I don't remember exactly how I got him up, but somehow I did, and I got his body to shore. By now, there were people there, cops, and everyone, so I just let them handle the rest of it.

As we previously told you in "Winegar Reflections," probably the saddest loss was that of little Bobbie Lahaie, who drowned in Little Horsehead Lake on December 1st, 1951. He was just seven years old.

I was trappin' that day, and the ice had just frozen out there, so it was pretty thin. Bobbie Lahaie's family lived right by the lake, and he went walking out on the ice. His mother said he was singing, "I Sail My Ship Alone.."

Note: This was a country song written and performed by Moon Mullican in 1950. Singer Hank Williams later popularized it.

He went out on that thin ice, and the ice gave way beneath his feet, and he went through. I guess he thought that, because there was ice all over, that he could walk anywhere out there. I came past there a short time later, maybe ten minutes or so and I heard his mother screaming what happened. I backed up my jeep and loaded up my little 8 ft pram, I put the pram in the water and pushed it out there. I got out to where he had gone in, but he was already gone. He was lying face down on the bottom of the lake, with his arms and legs all spread out. I used one of the oars and tipped him up so I could get ahold of him. Somehow I got him to shore. By that time, the Vilas County cops had arrived and were waiting there. Once I got him up to them, they took it from there. Of course, by then, everyone in town was out there. People were saying, "Chet saved him!" But no, I didn't save him, I just brought him in.

As you can see, Chet was involved in not only saving others from drowning, but he also was responsible for the recovery of the bodies of those who had not been able to make it out of the water alive.

But, out of all of the people he helped, there was one person that, if Chet had not been the man he is, would not have survived his near-drowning experience, and that would have made this book impossible....

I was out checking my trap lines and was cutting across the point on Big Horsehead. I had walked to my mink set, at the spring hole there. It was an ideal spot for trapping mink, since it would not freeze up.

I was walking over there and, of course, I was sliding my feet on the ice. There was no snow on the ice and it was only about an inch or two thick. I could see that the ice was cracking, but I was so used to walking on cracked ice that it never bothered me. So, even though the ice was cracking, I kept going and checked my set, and started back the same route.

This is where I made my mistake and learned a valuable lesson. I never should have walked back the same way, over that already cracked ice. That was about the closest I ever came to drowning. The ice broke and I fell through. I had my hip boots on, and I couldn't touch the bottom.

I was able to push myself up a little and got my hands on the ice. That ice was as smooth as window glass. There was nothing to hang on to. It was about then that I also learned that I should have been carrying a couple of ice picks.

Boy, I had one hell of a time getting out. I said to myself, "Chester, if you want to make it and if you want to live a little longer, you better kick like a son of a bitch right now!" I knew I had to get my legs up so I could get my body on the ice. By now my hip boots were full of water, and I had already been in the water for quite a while. I just kept working my hands on the ice, *and kicking my legs, and finally, I was able to get myself out and onto better ice.*

I rolled down my hip boots and drained the water out. But I still had to take them off before I got to the shore because my feet were just freezing. It okay walking on the ice like that, but when I got to land, there was no snow and the ground was frozen. My feet were so cold, and trying to walk on that rough ground, hurt like hell. So, I had to put my boots back on in order to walk to my jeep. I made it there and then had to drive back to town in that open jeep. I finally made it home and was able to dry out and warm up, but that was one close call.

The two things I learned from that incident was that I should always carry a couple of ice picks with me. And the most important lesson was that I should never, ever, walk back across ice that I had cracked already.

The Dumask family arrives in Winegar in 1934. Manda, Chester, Violet, Lambert, and father Ray. Soon, Ray was forced to go on the road looking for work as the sawmill shut down, and Manda was left to raise the three children.

Chet, age 15, catches his very first mink. He basically taught himself how to trap, since not many of the so called "experts" were able or willing to give him any help.

Home from the Navy and standing by his first car. Even though he enlisted for the "duration of the war" in 1944, the war ended just 15 months later. When asked what ship he was on, Chet's reply is "I was on the USS Never Sailed"

Chet with the black bear he killed for his good friend, Harry Peters. For a few moments out in the woods, it was a toss-up as to who was the hunter and who was the hunted. Luckily for Chet, the bear gave up before he did.

Gunnar Larson, a life-long friend of Chet. Gunnar owned the Winegar Tavern, which was built across the street from the pool hall which was torn down after the mill moved out. Chet's mother, Manda, worked for Gunnar, and the lived together. Manda and Gunnar are buried side by side in Evergreen Cemetery.

For years, Chet and his family owned an operated a business, selling bait, sporting goods, outboard motors and snowmobiles.

Wiley E. Coyote. Chet trapped and killed scores of these cowardly, but dangerous, animals throughout his trapping career, which spanned over seventy years.

You might say that Chet, using the trap set-up shown here, clearly "out-foxed" this one.

Chet and his three boys, Mitch, Mark, and Marty, shown with a whole lot of beaver hides, along with coyotes, and foxes.

One of the many, many coyotes that Chet caught. Other trappers would shoot their catch, but Chet had a different, and less messy way of dispatching his prey. He suffocated them so as not to disturb his set, and therefore was able to re-use it.

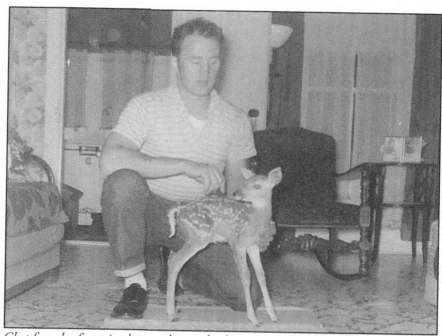

Chet found a fawn in the woods near his home, so he brought it home to show his sons. He then took it back to the same spot where he found it and released it.

It sure looks like the boys are enjoying this short visit.

Two of the many dogs that Chet has owned, Nip and Tuck. Chet has always had a special relationship with his dogs and if you see them together, the love and respect between them is readily apparent. As a side note, Chet actually rescued Tuck, who had fallen through the ice near Chet's home. At the time, Chet was a young 84 yr. old.

Just one of the hundreds of beaver that Chet has trapped in his lifetime. He finally retired from trapping them when after his 92nd birthday. He said he would let some of the younger guys have all the fun now....

Who else, but Chet Dumask, would even think to try and catch not one, but two beaver, at the same time, with his bare hands?

After showing the beaver to people around the town, Chet ended up releasing them back where they were caught, so that chapter had a happy ending.

This fisher does not look happy that Chet is taking his picture. A fisher is related to the weasel but has been known to act more like a wolverine.

In a single day, Chet not only caught Wiley, but caught the entire Coyote family.

Chet, Louie Auchter, and the tire iron used to kill this coyote.

This what the garage of a successful trapper looks like!

Chet has the truck loaded with pelts and is ready to head to the buyer. When he was a teen-ager, the buyers would come to his house, because they knew he would always have quality pelts for them.

Chet is shown here sharing some of his trapping stories with local students.

Looks like Chet caught the 'missing Lynx'

Chet shows off his catch at the local Presque Isle bar.

CHAPTER EIGHT
Friendships

"After that, he shot at every one of the deer when they were running, and you know where he hit them? Right in the head!"

At the end of Winegar's logging boom in the 1930s, the owners of the sawmill mill moved their operation to Lake Linden, MI. The residents of Winegar were devastated by this move because almost all of them depended on the mill for their livelihood. As the money dried up, so did the population of the tiny town. One of the businesses' that was affected by the absence of clientele was the town's pool hall, located on Main St. in the center of town. Most people do not know that the pool hall, in a way, would have a second life. You see, when the building was condemned and torn down, the lumber was used to build a bar directly across the street. This bar was known as the "Winegar Tavern" and was owned by one Gunnar Larsen. (the bar is still there, and today it is known as the "Yacht Club.")

Gunnar and Chet had a long and lasting friendship. They relied on each other for help when needed and spent many hours together. Just as I am sure that Chet learned some life lessons from Gunnar, I am confident that Gunnar learned some valuable skills from Chet also.

Gunnar Larsen was a good man, and he would help out anybody who needed help in that town. If anyone came in and was down on their luck, they could count on Gunnar to borrow them the money. After my mom and I got in there with Gunnar, the townspeople didn't like it very well, especially the women.

I used to tend bar for Gunnar sometimes, like when he went to eat at my mother's house across the street from the bar. And that is how my mother got into running that bar down on Hwy W, because Gunnar bought that bar from John McGee, and needed someone to operate it. Then, later on, he sold the bar to Mary and Axel Olssen and their son, Holger.

I had first started with Gunnar when Jack Finnegan and I set up a bait stand by his tavern in the middle of town. Art

McCarty was the bait man. Jack and I would catch the minnows and take them over to the stand. We sold minnows there for a long time; then we moved the stand down to the bottom of the hill where Chick Spenser had the gas station (now called Karsyn's Korner). But it didn't work out that well down there, so we moved it back up by Gunnar's. Gunnar liked it there by the bar because it brought in a lot of guys. Later on, Frances Graham, who had the hardware store just down the street, wanted to sell the store, but I didn't have enough money to buy it. I went to Gunnar, and I said, "I know Frances wants to sell the place, but I need to know if I can borrow the money to buy it." He said, "Yes, you can, Chet." So, I got the money and bought the place.

And I told Frances, "Now, if you want, we can go in the morning, down to Eagle River, and I'll pay you there, and we will make the deal. But don't tell nobody about this." The reason I told her that was because, if some of these nosy women around town found out about it, they would try to stop her from selling to me, just out of spite. I was right about them too. When we had the store, not one of them would ever set foot in the place. That was how much they hated us.

I took Gunnar out hunting a lot. I would even make him his stand- a great big Evinrude cardboard box, and he could sit inside there with a little heater. It was a pretty good deal for him. The first deer he shot out of there was a six-point buck, but he never dropped it until it was way behind him. I asked him, "Gunnar, how the hell come you didn't shoot him. You watched him go all the way around you like that, and then you finally shot him."

Gunnar said, "Well, he was runnin', and he didn't stop until he got back around there." I said that was OK, and told him that, "You have to start shooting at them when they are running." After that, he shot at every one of the deer when they were running, and you know where he hit them? Right in the head! I could never figure that out, but I wouldn't say anything. I just thought to myself, "Well, at least he is killing them, and as long as the horns don't fall off, that was OK."

I asked Chet where was the best place to shoot the deer, and this was his explanation:

Well, nobody would shoot them where I shot them. I shoot 'em in the neck. I like the neck- the base of the neck where it enters the body. Just ahead of the front shoulders. That's where I shoot them. Everybody else wants to shoot them in the heart, just behind the front shoulders. But when I shoot them in the neck, "BAM," they go down just like that! The other guys shoot them behind the shoulder, and the damn deer will run for a ways before they drop. I mean, if you heart shoot them, they will sometimes go for about 100 yards before they fall.

I worked with Gunnar and eventually taught him how to be a pretty darn good hunter. I would tell him where to stand and watch. He would sometimes go out by himself, and he liked to walk a lot, so I let him go. I did take him hunting with me out by Henry Fromm's mink farm. Henry had told me, "Chet, you can hunt this land just like it is your own. You hunt, and fish and trap on it like it is your own." He liked me because I used to give him all my beaver carcasses to feed to his mink. I would pull in there by him, with a load of beaver carcasses, and he would have a big 'ol smile on his face. He liked Gunnar too, so we could always go out there. There were three guys from Boulder Junction who acted like they owned the whole area. Well, when Henry Fromm let Gunnar and I hunt in there, these guys started to raise a little hell, so Henry ran them out of there altogether.

We fished a lot together too. Gunnar and I were good friends with Mickey Green, who had some slot machines in Gunnar's bar, and since he also owned all the Lone Pine area east of town, we could fish out there. We were out there one time, and Gunnar says, "I want you to get me a set-up just like the spinning deal you are using." At that time, I had the store, and I could set up any rig the way I wanted. I could cast into those lily pads and hook a bass, and I could haul them right through the pads.

But Gunnar couldn't do that. So I rigged him up with a good rod and reel, and I put a 10-12 pound test line on it. He had been listening to all the know-nothings in the bar, who were telling him that he should use a real light line. Well, when he would use that line, he was always breaking it. I finally told him, "That don't work, Gunnar. The fish don't care whether the line is heavy or light; they are just after the bait. If you use a light line, they are just going to break it and be gone."

Gunnar listened to me, and I fixed him up the right way. He really liked that, and from then on, he started catching a lot more fish.

There was another guy in town, who I won't name, but he was a worse fisherman than Gunnar. He was a mess. I told him, "You either fish the way I tell you, or I am not going with you!". I didn't have time for that crap. See, Gunnar would listen to me, but this guy wouldn't, so I left him to figure it out on his own. I don't know if he ever did.

Just east of town a little ways is the boat landing at Little Horsehead Lake. Two large culverts run under County Hwy B and empty into the lake. It is a perfect spot to fish. I fished off those culverts once with Inez Eschenbauch. I was catching walleyes left and right, and she wasn't catching anything. She was getting pretty mad at me. She said, "Let me fish where you are!" So I let her. I moved farther down, and I was still catching *fish, and she wasn't. So she was really pissed at me. That is what I mean- you can't win for losin'.*

But that was the talent I had. If I weren't catching anything, I would do something about it!. I would just keep on changing things until I started catching them. And I was reeling in them walleyes left and right, right next to where she was not even getting a nibble. I didn't do it to be mean. I just knew how to fish better than she did.

Another activity that Chet and Gunnar helped each other with was the harvesting and storing of ice in Gunnar's icehouse, built next to his tavern. This was in the days before the widespread use of electric refrigeration. Here are a few ice house cubes of information…

Icehouses were buildings used to store ice throughout the year, commonly used before the invention of the refrigerator. Some were underground chambers, usually man-made, close to natural sources of winter ice such as freshwater lakes, but many were buildings with various types of insulation.

Harvesting ice was cold, hard, wet work. At times, it was dangerous too. Once the first piece of ice was cut, a man could easily fall into the freezing water and drown. And in the process of storing the ice, a man could be crushed by a falling cake of ice which, as you will see, could have easily happened to Gunnar one day.

A thick layer of sawdust or salt hay was layered on the floor of the icehouse before the ice arrived. The ice blocks were pushed up a plank into the house and layered inside with a thick layer of sawdust that kept the cakes separated when taken out during the summer. About a foot of sawdust or hay was used between the ice and the walls of the ice house for insulation. After the house was filled with the ice blocks, a layer of sawdust or hay was spread on the top layer as well.

As home and business refrigeration became more commonplace, ice houses fell into disuse, and the home ice delivery business declined until it had virtually disappeared by the late 1960s.

I also used to help Gunnar with the ice house he had next to the tavern. We packed ice there every year, and that was quite a job. Most of the time, he got the ice off of Little Horsehead Lake because it was so close. Frank Jirikowic would cut it for him. He had a motorcycle frame, and he put a big sawblade on the rear wheel. And he fixed up the handlebars on that so he could steer it. He was a genius when it came to that sort of stuff. Frank sawed the ice for all the people around here, and then he went up to Lake Gogebic, and he cut for different places up there. Billy

Kunschke and I would go with him. He liked us because we were good workers for him.

We would have a conveyor set up with a little 'putt-putt' motor on it, and Frank would cut the ice, but he would never cut it all the way through. He would cut almost all the way through the ice, except for about the last four inches, so we could still walk on it. Then we could bust it apart with pinch bars, break the blocks off, and put them on the conveyor and up they would go to the truck. Frank would drive the truck to the ice house, and we would push the blocks off there. It was about the same process to unload the ice, but that was all by hand; there was no machine work there. We just had a wooden slide with side rails there to pull them up, since there was no conveyor belt. When we got the blocks into the ice house, we used snow to pack them in. We would have to shovel snow up into there and pack it between each block., and also in between each layer. Because of some melting, we would end up losing the top half of the top row most times. This would happen even though we would put 8-12 inches of sawdust on top of the blocks.

The blocks were cut into 12-inch squares, and then to whatever depth the ice was. Frank usually liked to cut to about an 18-20 inch ice depth. Most of the time, Frank would load the truck by himself, but Bill Kunschke and I would help unload at the ice house. When the truck would get to the ice house, we would throw a rope down the ramp, and haul the blocks up.

That is how Gunnar broke his leg one time. He was down at the bottom, putting the rope around the blocks, and we would pull them up. That one time, he put the rope to close to the top of the ice block. We were pulling the ice block up, and when it got halfway up, it tipped over. The ice block slid back down the ramp, and Gunnar tried to jump out of the way. He ended up falling backward and actually sat on his leg and broke it! I loaded him in my car and took him to the hospital in Wakefield.

Later on, Gunnar decided he didn't want the bar anymore, and he surprised Chet by offering to GIVE him the business.

I could have got the bar for nothing! I could have got it and sold it if I wanted to. But that wouldn't be right. I turned him down.

He was surprised at that. "You don't want to own the bar?" he asked me.

"Nope."

"Why not?"

"Because I don't want to drink."

"You don't want to drink?"

"No, Gunnar, I just don't want to drink. And if you run a bar, the customers are going to expect you to drink with them. If

you don't, eventually they will stop coming in." Even when I just bartended there, if they offered me a drink, I just said no. Plus, I was an outdoors type of guy anyway, and I didn't want to be inside all that much.

Anyway, Gunnar ended up selling the bar to Clyde and Laverne Alho. He and my mom went to live in Arizona, and he remained there until his death in 1976. I took care of all his funeral arrangements, including getting his body returned here and burying him in Evergreen Cemetery. He had three sisters, and they came for the funeral. I had a lawyer from Manitowish Waters handle the probate and get that all settled.

When my mother passed away in 1994, I had her buried alongside Gunnar at Evergreen.

CHAPTER NINE
My Three Sons

"The main thing that I believe I taught my three boys was, "If you do something, do it right. If you do that, you will always have work!"

Carl Wolter told me that one of the ways you can tell the character of a man is to look at his children. If that is the measuring stick for Chet, then he is one hell of a man. Chey has three sons, Mitch, Mark, and Marty. All three have grown up to be hard-working, successful, family men. Unfortunately for me, they were all working so hard, that I barely had time to talk to them about this book.

Mitch was out of state at the time of this writing, but before he left, he did indicate that, when his dad had the store in Presque Isle, Mitch did a lot of work there, repairing outboard motors and whatever else his dad needed him to do. As he grew up, he learned to be a heavy equipment operator and a very good one at that. Chet told me that there isn't a piece of equipment around that Mitch can't operate.

I did get to speak to Mark at the American Legion Post one night, and I asked him to tell me two things that his dad taught him, that he still uses today. His response was simple.

"He taught me never to trust anybody, and never to tell anybody anything."

Our conversation was short, but that sentence spoke volumes about Chet's upbringing and how he needed to live in order to provide for his family.

Chet explained that philosophy to me-

"The reason I taught them that was because of what I went through here. And not with just one bunch, it was with almost anybody that you dealt with back then. You just don't assume that a guy is honest; they have to prove that to you. I learned

that from both my mother and also from Roy Sipps. So, it would really take a lot for me to trust anybody."

I was able to have a phone conversation with Chet's youngest son, Marty, who lives in the Wausau, WI area. Here are his answers to my questions:

If you could go back and re-experience one adventure that you had with your dad that you remember fondly, what would it be? Or any other fun things that you and he did together that you look back on.

"Legally?" he asked, with a laugh.

"Doesn't have to be."

"A couple of things come to mind. I do remember that when I was in 7ᵗʰ or 8ᵗʰ grade, my dad and I used to sneak across the state line into Michigan, to go ice fishing on few lakes over there.

The first thing you would have to do is to make sure that you don't leave any tracks behind. That was part of the trapper in Dad. We would use our snowshoes to kind of sweep over the snow to obliterate our tracks.

I remember going to fish this one lake that we had fished numerous times, and I saw a car coming down the road. I had my snowshoes on. Back then, we didn't have the high-tech snowshoes that they have today. The ones we had were the long teardrop wooden ones. I saw that car, and I started running for a balsam tree to hide under. A kid trying to run in those snowshoes was not easy! Somehow I managed to roll up under the tree and hide. I don't know how I did that, but they drove by and were none the wiser. Gunnar Larson was with us that day, and I remember my dad bragging to him about how good I had hidden. He was real proud of me, how I got under that tree and hid so quickly.

Another time, when I was about 15-16 years old, we were again sneaking into Michigan, since it was right next door. We were trapping some minnows, trying to get some chubs out of those streams over there. We were using glass traps; it was one of our first times using the glass traps.

We were in this little creek that was loaded with chubs, and we were experimenting with these new traps. We would set some traps, then go up and sit on the bank, and then go back in and check them. Those traps were just loaded with chubs! We were really successful at trapping the chubs. Then we had to sneak back out of there and get back into Wisconsin.

Along with those chubs, we also got us a few nice trout at the same time. I saw those trout, and I thought they were pretty *cool. And that is what got me started on trout fishing, and I am a big trout fisherman today because of that.*

We had snuck in there, and somehow we ended up running into Clyde Alho, who was a big trout fisherman. He was on that stream fishing as we were coming out with all these chubs. We made a truce between us that "mums the word", and that neither of us would say anything about that spot to anyone. I always wanted to pick Clyde's brain about trout fishing, but, unfortunately, I never got the opportunity."

Tell me about how your dad helped you get started in trapping.

My brother, Mitch, trapped a little in the beginning but then got away from it, and I don't believe Mark trapped at all. One the other hand, I kind of grabbed onto it right away. I remember being in 7ᵗʰ and 8ᵗʰ grade running a little trap line, less than a dozen traps, along the river by Presque Isle. I would have to check them every morning before getting on the school bus. Later on, I got into trapping by the ponds and the cattails. Then I would probably have 30-40 traps there.

I remember that one time I checked my traps and I said "Hey, look! I caught a mink!"

Later on, I asked Chet about this, and he explained what really happened....

"Marty was into trapping for awhile. One time, he set a trap, and when he left for school, I went out and put a mink in the trap. He was so excited when he thought he caught his first mink. I did it to help get him started and to keep him interested...."

Marty continues:

Every fall, I took a week off of school, and we would run the trap lines. It didn't matter if my teachers approved it or not; I still took that week off. My dad taught me how to skin the muskrats and stretch the hides.

I haven't trapped now for years, but I am getting close to retirement, and I would really like to get back into it.

Do you ever remember a time when your dad just gave up on something; just threw his hands in the air and said, "I quit. I can't do this..."

"No. I never saw Dad do that. If he tried something and it didn't work, he kept at it, kept changing things, and trying again until it did work. And I feel the same way. I think you always have to be observant and be open to learning new things. I have come across that many times in my life. There are always

different ways of doing things, and if you can learn to merge some of them together, you can succeed.

I played basketball in high school, and I coached it for sixteen years at the high school here in Wausau, and while doing that, I learned to try new things in that as well. I also coached baseball for two years here.

List three things that Chet taught you as a boy that you still use today.

"Work ethic. He was always big on work. You have to have work, he would say. And do a good job and do it right.

Dad also taught me how to make maple syrup. I have one maple tree here in my yard, and I made twelve pints of syrup last year. I remember in grade school, getting off the bus in mid-March, and having to run down to the state line with him in his Jeep CJ, where he owned land, and we would gather the sap. We would bring that sap home and fire up the cooker. Syrup season would usually last about a month, depending on the weather. A few years ago, I did show my brother Mark and his wife Kim, how to make it.

I guess the other thing that I learned from him would be a combination of the whole outdoor experience. The hunting, fishing, trapping, and even the maple sap gathering were very memorable to me. Part of that, of course, had to do with the area in which we lived. If you lived in Presque Isle- you did outdoor things. So I learned a lot of the outdoor stuff from him, and then I figured out some more things on my own, and it has worked out well."

Trying to do things with your dad can be trying at times. (I know this from my experiences with my dad as well). Fathers can be difficult when trying to teach their sons, and sometimes it doesn't go as well as it could. How much of your dad do you see in yourself? How much do you feel that you and your dad are alike?

"I guess there is good and bad with that. Dad could have a temper at times. I try to keep a check on my anger. I have seen how he reacts to some things, and I don't want to react that way, so I try to think it through before I act.

On the other hand, like him, I have gotten really good at gardening. He got me into gardening when I was in grade school. I had my own garden, separate from his, and I would grow a few tomato plants. I still have a nice garden today, and sometimes I now bring vegetables up to him."

I have seen Chet's sons grow from boys to men (albeit from a distance), and I would certainly agree with what Carl Wolter said at the beginning of this chapter. They all appear to be excellent men, and I am confident, from my many conversations with Chet, that he is incredibly proud of each of them.

CHAPTER TEN

Going to the Dogs

"That was my Duke. He was a good dog."

It has been said that dogs are a "man's best friend," but it is also true that a man can be his dog's best friend as well. I don't think that the relationship between the two could ever be better illustrated than by showing the powerful bond that Chet shared with each of his beloved dogs. To see them together is to bear witness to the mutual love, caring, and respect that they have for each other.

I once had a Springer Spaniel, named Jack. He had the big ears, hanging down, you' know. He was a good dog. I think he just got old and died.

I had another one that I named Brandy. He was a real big Golden Retriever. He got to be 11-12 years old. We came home from the Legion one night, and he was layin' down and couldn't get up. So, I had to take him to the Vet to be put down. The Vet gave him a shot and put him down. I buried him up on the hill up here by my garden, so he could always be "King of the Hill!"

Then I had a couple more, named Nip and Tuck. They are buried in my apple orchard here. I got them both right around the same time, Peggy Johnson got me one. I had put Brandy down and got Nip; then, she gave me Tuck, so now I had two dogs. I didn't want to have two dogs at the same time, but I didn't want her to get mad, so I kept both of them. They were both Golden retrievers, like Brandy.

Trigger was a chocolate Lab that I had. Out at the lake (Presque Isle), there is a forty-foot long pier. When I would take Trigger out there, he would run the whole length of that pier and leap into the water. He was around 85 lbs. Boy, he really made a huge splash. He could jump high too. I put a pad on the end of the pier so he would not slip if the wood were wet. Oh, he enjoyed doing that. I would only let him do that a few times, though, because I didn't want him to hurt himself.

Chet and I spent a lot of time talking about his dogs. He truly loved every one of them, and I am sure that, when the time came, and they died, those were some sorrowful times for him. But there was the death of one dog, Duke (not the current one that lives with him now), that still sparks a tremendous amount of emotion and deep sadness from Chet. Here is what he told me:

I had gone to Milwaukee for Evinrude school for two weeks when I had the store. When I was away like that, my dog, Duke, would go uptown looking for me. He should have been kept on a leash, but for some reason, that time he was running free.

When I got home, the first thing I asked my wife was, "Where's Duke?"

She said, "Oh, he died."

"Duke died? What happened?"

She said, "Bill Newberry buried him."

"Well, how come he died?" She said that she didn't know how he died, only that he was dead, and Bill Newberry had buried him. She knew what had happened, but she didn't want to tell me, because she was afraid of what I might do.

I didn't get to go over to Bill Newberry's house, but for some reason or another, I went up by the landfill. I looked down in the pit, and there was my dog laying down there! I went down in that pit, and I picked Duke up.

I said, "I got to re-bury you, buddy. I don't want you rottin' in the dump. "

I took him, and I went over by the fence that separated the town dump from the Presque Isle Cemetery. I dug a hole right tight to the fence, inside the cemetery. I put him in there, and I covered him up.

Then, that damn Milon Mackenzie said something about a dog in the cemetery, so they dug him up, and I don't know what they did with him.

I found out a little bit later that Harold "Zip" Zippro, the town cop at the time, shot my dog. He was going with Mae Prosser then, and she had a little ankle-biter dog. She was afraid to let her dog out for fear that the big dogs would get after it. Apparently, Zippro thought it would be a good idea to "eliminate" some of those bigger dogs. I wanted to go after Zippro, but I held off. But it still pisses me off that the son of a bitch murdered my dog. I also found out that he had shot and killed Jerry Hartmann's dog, and Jerry sued him and got $500 out of him. I let it go, but I never forgot. It still bothers me to this day.

That was my Duke. He was a good dog.

Chet also shared a story with me about how he saved one of his dogs from drowning in the river by his house. This incident happened around the time that Chet was 84 years old.

I had the two dogs then, Nip and Tuck. There was a fox that would come around every night and tease the dogs. It was just a pattern. Then the dogs would start barking like crazy.

Well, this one night, the fox was out there, and I was in the house, but I could only hear one dog barking. So, I went outside with the flashlight, and I shined it around. I saw Nip in the yard. I kept shining the light around, and I saw a pair of eyes out there in the open water. There was ice along the edges, but the middle of the river had open water. And there was Tuck, out there in the water with his front paws on the edge of the ice. It was too deep for him to touch bottom there, and he couldn't get up onto the ice.

I knew that if I tried to walk on that thin ice, I would fall through, so I laid down and slid over close to him. Of course, when you grab hold of him by the nape of the neck, you can't pull him because his chest would be hitting the ice edge. I knew that I would have to turn him on his side, and when I did that, I was able to pull him right up onto the ice.

We mentioned in an earlier chapter that Chet not only saved people from drowning and recovered the bodies of those who couldn't be saved, and you can now also credit him saving the life of one of his furry best friends.

CHAPTER ELEVEN
He Fought the Law

People asked if that was "out of season?" But it wasn't. In those days, you could shoot a bear most anytime.

***NOTE: Killing animals out of season is against the law. But, by some people living on hard times in rural America, it was not considered violating. If you needed meat for your family, you went out and got some, no matter what time of the year it was. It wasn't violating- it was subsistence....

Me and Buddy Merrick, we killed a lot of deer. Just about once a week, we would shoot a deer and take half apiece. I would have half for my family, and he would have half for his.

One time his dad, Butch Merrick, lost his 30-30 rifle to the damn game wardens. See, we used to go across the big dam just north of town and go back in there and shoot deer. That was when we would go on foot, you know. Before that, we would just shoot out of the car, mostly along the Crab Lake road. Anyway, we shot a deer that was really close to the Michigan line. And the Michigan deer season was open then. I was up there with him, and here come this guy coming from the Michigan side. He called to us, saying "Hey! Wait a minute! I'm lost! I'm lost!" I told him, "Well, you hear that sound over there? You follow that sound, and it'll take you right into Winegar." "Well," he says, "Wait for me!" I told Merrick, "Oh no! We're out of here! That's a game warden!" And it was. It was a Michigan game warden. So we took off, and then we looked back, and he was trying to catch up to us, but we knew he couldn't. No, we were too fast on our feet! Ya, he wanted to nail us, but we got out of that one real quick.

I spent a lot of time with Jack McGlinn, but after a while, I quit violatin' with him. He wasn't a good violator. He would get all shook up, and panic. And when we would have to shoot, that echo would go out all over the place and make us pretty easy to spot.

I saw the game warden from Boulder Junction, Ben Bendrick, looking for somebody that one time. And I was the guy he was lookin' for! But I was trapping at the time, and wasn't out there shootin", so he couldn't do anything.

Bendrick has checked my truck two different times when he saw me parked, and I was checking my sets. He comes along, he and his partner, and they go through my truck. And he says to me, "No gun?" I said, "Nope." He told me, "I thought you'd have a shotgun to shoot some birds." I said, "Ben, If I carried that shotgun, that would be all I was doing was shootin' birds. But I am trapping now, and I don't have the gun, and I don't want the gun. Because, sure, I could shoot a lot of birds. I could clean this country out, because I run the same route every day, every day." He liked that, and kind of complimented me on that. I said, if I want to go huntin' birds, I'll go bird huntin'. But I'm not huntin' birds right now- I'm trapping'." And that's the way it worked. I think he liked that about me.

Presque Isle Warden....

This guy, who was a game warden at the time, wanted me to go deer huntin' with him out next to Hwy B. This bow hunting. Well, I shot a deer with the bow and arrow, and I dropped him right there. I hit him, and he made just one lunge and dropped. He says, "We'll leave it and come back later." I told him, "That's the worst thing a violater can do. I would never have shot that deer, but you wanted me too." When you are driving along, and you come to an opening like this where the deer are, almost every time you would see one. And that's where a warden is going to be watchin'. He is going to be watchin', and he is going to let you shoot it. Then, he is going to wait until you come to pick it up.

So, he says to me, "You want to pick it up?" I said, "Hell, no! You wanted me to shoot it. If you want it picked up, you do it. You are going to have to go pick it up all by yourself. I knew that he was just trying to get me pinched. He knew he could get away with it, and I would be the one who had to take the rap.

I never got pinched for violatin' in my life (except that time with Jack McGlinn). I had the wardens question me, but they couldn't ever pinch me.

Fighting with A Michigan game warden...

I was trappin' minnows with Jack McGlinn just across the state line one day.

There was an old road alongside this river in Michigan, off the Palmer Rd, and we were trappin' minnows in there. I drove down the road, which really was just a couple of ruts, but that was the only place we could catch any redtails. At that time, there were no redtails around here, so we would sneak over there once in a while. Well, McGlinn wasn't a very good guy to violate with. He was kind of looney. He couldn't figure out anything about how to do things and not get caught.

I dropped him off at one spot so he could check a half dozen traps, and I drove down to the end of the grade, where there used to be an old wooden bridge across the river, from years ago for the logging trucks and such. I had a half dozen traps to check in there. I would go down there and empty the traps and put the minnows in my car. I had bought this here 1949 car, which had a huge trunk, and I could put the minnow tank in there. I could close the trunk, and no one would be able to see that tank full of minnows at all. This was the first time I used that car for hauling minnows.

Of course, I wanted to drive down that road and check first, because the game wardens would sometimes sit down there and wait for you to drive in. You see, they would check those old dirt roads for tracks of any cars that had driven there. Then, they would hide and wait for you so that they could pinch you. But McGlinn talked me out of doin' that.

"No, no," he says, "They won't be down there. Let's just get done. I want to get back home." That was his idea! Don't use any of my ideas, cuz I don't know nuthin', or so he thought. He's the smart guy! He was wrong about everything that day.

Anyway, I dropped him off and drove down to the end of the road. I went and got my minnows out of the traps and put them in the tank in my car. As I got in the car, all of a sudden, I saw movement in my mirror. It was them two game wardens.

They came up by the car, one by the driver's side door and the other one by the door on the other side. Their names were Ainsley and Bowmaster. Bowmaster was the game warden from Bessemer, and Ainsley was from Marinesco.

Both car doors were open at the time and I had the key in the ignition. It was just a single key, nothing else hanging on it.

Ainsley told me, "Get Out!"

I asked, "What for?"

"Never mind! Get out!"

I asked, "Who are you?"

"Never mind. Get out!"

I says, "No! I'm not getting out for you."

Ainsley then grabbed my leg and my arm, so he got my left side out, but I had my right knee by the steering column, and that was blocking him from pulling me out of the car. But I still had my hand free. If that dam Bowmaster had been smart, he would have just reached in on the right side and pushed me out. But he didn't do that.

He said to Ainsley, "I'll show you how to get him out of there, John!"

Ainsley let go of my leg and my arm, and Bowmaster reached in and grabbed me by my testicles! Well, when he did that, I pulled his head in, and I hit that son of a gun three or four times, just as hard as I could. POW! POW! POW! And the more I hit him, the more he pulled his head down, and I was able to hit him high, but I did get both of his eyes shut! By now, the State cops had arrived, and they had to hold him up to walk him out. You see, they called the state cops before they tried to grab me because my car didn't have a license plate. But, I had ordered the plates, so I was ok with the state cops.

Anyway, the state cops came in, and they looked at Bowmaster and then looked at me, and one of them got a big smile on his face. I figured that I was ok then.

Of course, by now, McGlinn had disappeared. He ran and ran and ran. He told me later, "I ran so hard, when I saw Bunn Cole go by in his jeep up on that other road, I was so out of breath I couldn't even holler.

I was pretty upset with him because all he would have had to do was come along the river and warn me that there were wardens up there. Had he done that, I wouldn't have come up there with a bucket of minnows.

The end of it was I had to go to court and pay fines. Judge Dechelbar was the judge at the time, and he fined me $50 for trapping the minnows, and another $50 for giving Bowmaster two black eyes. It was worth the $50 for giving him the black eyes! And, you know what? I would do the same thing to him today if I had the chance....

CHAPTER TWELVE
Beaver Tales

"I was holdin' that beaver by the tail, and he was really fightin'! He rattled me up and down like a window shade...!"

Chet has never been one to shy away from a challenge. He has been known to attempt things just to see if they could be done. That is why he has become such an accomplished trapper, hunter, fisherman, and all-around outdoorsman.

As outlined previously in this book, Chet has trapped hundreds, if not thousands of beaver, and has had many challenges along the way. The tale I am about to relate to you may seem by some to be somewhat beyond belief, but, if you know Chet, you would never doubt the truth of this particular catch (or, to be more accurate, catches)…

Before we get to that, let me share a few beaver facts with you so that you will be as informed as I am (which isn't much) about these animals….

According to Wikipedia, the beaver is the largest rodent in North America and the second-largest in the world. The body of the adult males averages 29-35 inches in length, plus another 10 inches when you factor in the tail. They weigh about 42 lbs, although some can be much heavier.

The beaver is located throughout North America and Canada.

Beavers are monogamous and therefore mate with the same beaver for life. They are mainly active at night and can stay underwater for up to 15 minutes. They can also swim up to 5 miles per hour.

North American Beavers are herbivores and therefore eat leaves, roots, aquatic plants, and bark. When a beaver chops a tree down, they will eat at the bark of the trunk but mainly want to get to the more tender branches at the top.

Now that you know almost all there is to know about this sizeable toothed rodent, let's let Chet tell us the story of how he caught not one, but two, beaver, at the same time….with his bare hands!

It was in the middle of the summer of 1949. I was going after some mud minnows. I was looking for some new ponds to set traps in. I came to this one pond, and I had a couple of minnow traps along with me. The pond was in between Oxbow Road going to Kunsche's resort, and Stateline Lake road.

There was a great big pine log lying down. It had broken off the tree and was sticking out in the water. I wanted to hang a minnow trap out near the end of that log. I hadn't set one like that, but I am a guy who likes to experiment a lot on how to catch something. When you do that, you will eventually learn the best way to trap whatever you are going after. Because I was willing to take the time to watch and learn the habits of whatever I was trapping, either animals or minnows, I was able to get good at catching all of them. I used to find a hell of a lot of mud minnows because I learned their habits.

I was walking out on this log, and I got almost to the end of it when I heard the "SLAP!" of a beaver tail hitting the water! I said, "There's a darn beaver by this log." I watched him go down, and I see the fizz of his air bubbles. And he stopped there. I said, "I'll catch the son of a gun, or at least I'll trap him."

So, I eased off the log, and the water came over my hip boots, and it only took about one step to get to where he was. I reached down the, and my head was under the water. I touched him very lightly on the hump of his back and tippy-toed my fingers down toward his tail. Right where his tail attaches to his body, it is narrow there. I grabbed ahold of him, and Oh boy, let me tell you! He gave me a heck of a vibration! It was like about a hundred mile an hour wind on a window shade. He was rattlin' and rattlin', and I was hanging on to him. He weighed about 40-50 lbs. I finally got my other hand down there to help me out. I got off that log, and I was already soaking wet, so I just walked along the side of the log towards the shore.

About fifteen feet from shore, all of a sudden, there was another splash right there. I figured that that was probably the female over there. Well, the closer I got to her, the quieter the male that I was holding became. I saw where she went down, and now I could hold the male by one hand since he had calmed down, and I worked my way toward her. I reached down and grabbed the female beaver the same way I had caught the male. Now, I've got a beaver in each hand! I got them up on shore, and they were just like kittens. No problem! I wanted to put them in the trunk of my car, a 1949 Chevy that I had just bought. And to do that, I would need to get the key out of the ignition to unlock the trunk. But, I had a beaver in each hand! To this day, I don't remember how I managed to get the key and open the trunk, but somehow I did. I got the trunk lid open, and I put the two of them in there.

I drove into town and showed them to people, and everyone was saying, "Oh, you have to go show them to so and so!" I had them with me all day long and showed them to everyone. Herman Grasskamp told me, "When you get done playin' around with them, would you put them in the river behind my place? I would like them to build a dam there." At that time, he had those little cabins down below the hill, just north of town, heading to the Michigan line. He wanted high water down there. I told him I would let them go down there, but I didn't. I lied to him. I put them back where I caught them. I thought, "They ain't done nothing to me, so I am just going to put them back.

Wow, that was pretty amazing! I would not suggest that any of you "try this at home...."

But it certainly wasn't only beaver, mink, and minnows that Chet trapped. Next up is Chet's encounters with coyotes....

CHAPTER THIRTEEN

The Not So "Wiley" Coyote

I told Louie, "Stop! Stop the car! I want to catch that S.O.B!"

I have a question for anyone reading this book. Are you, or anyone you know, a fan of the coyote? I am going to guess that the answer is "No." The coyote is not a popular animal by any means. Their relatives, the wolf, fox, dog, and even jackals, are thought better of than the coyote. Here are just a few coyote facts and statistics:

1) They are basically a cowardly animal and are actually only dangerous if they are in a group. Rarely will they ever attack anything if they are alone. The only prey they will hunt alone is small mammals, birds, and mice. If the prey is more substantial, such a whitetail deer, they will only hunt them in packs.

2) They have few natural predators, such as bears, wolves, and mountain lions.

3) While you occasionally will spot them during daylight hours, they are mostly nocturnal and will hunt at night.

4) Coyotes have excellent vision and a keen sense of smell. They are also very swift and can achieve speeds of 40 mph

5) They will rarely attack humans, but if you encounter them, do not try to run away, or they will think you are prey. Stand your ground, and they should slink off like the cowards they are.

It is easy now to gather all this information from the internet, but men like Chet Dumask had to learn about them and all the other animals and rodents they wanted to catch through careful observation. They had to study how the coyote acted, and they had to learn his habits. Once armed with this information, they could then, and only then, become successful at trapping and killing them.

Now, as previously stated here, Chet taught himself to be one of the most successful trappers in the state. His observation powers were honed by the many hours he spent watching and studying whatever it was that he wanted to catch. It didn't matter if he was catching mud minnows or stalking a whitetail deer or black bear; Chet wanted to know everything he could about his prey.

But, back to the subject at hand, the Canis Latrans, or for those unfamiliar with the Latin designations, the North American coyote. I don't know if Chet has kept track of how many of these beasts he has dispatched, but I am sure that figure is very high, at least in the triple digits.

Here is Chet's version of two of his coyote encounters:

I was trapping out in the area between Rice Creek, and Big Crab Lake. We used to hunt deer back in there, and I always liked to get in there and take out those coyotes.

I caught a coyote in a trap, and he was pretty big. We were way back in the woods, and I didn't want to carry him or drag him out, so I thought that if I could get a noose around his neck, I could walk him out. He was still in the trap, and I was trying to lasso him. I was trying to get the rope on him, but he was jumping and snapping all the while.

Well, we kept dancing around, me trying to fake him out, and him snarlin' and snappin', and he then got lucky and bit me on my left hand. I still have the scar right here. I wrapped up my hand with my big red hanky. In the meantime, he had somehow got the trap loose from the stake and took off with it still attached to his foot. I saw him go over the hill and down into the swamp. I decided not to follow him in there, so I went around the edge of the swamp instead. He went through three different swamps before he got up on top of a hill by a big deer runway. I knew that when he got on that runway, he could really take off. I had to let him go that night, and I went home. I came back the next morning. He hadn't gone very much further than he had the night before. He just laid down and still had the trap and the chain hooked to hm. I was still pissed that he had bitten me, so I did something I didn't usually do; I shot him and drug him out of the woods.

Now, most of the coyotes I killed, I killed by suffocation. I rarely shot any of them. All the other guys would shoot the animals. You give them a tap enough that they are stunned, then you got free going. You put one foot on their throat, and the other foot on their ribcage and then they are done for. Most of the *other guys just shot the coyotes. You would see them walking around wearing their guns all the time, but not me.*

I used suffocation as a way to kill them because I didn't want any blood around the set. Or on my snowmobile in the wintertime. It would kind of screw up your set if there was blood there, so I wanted to keep the area clean. If I just suffocated them, then the area around the set was still pure, and I could again use the same set. In fact, it improved the set, and that was my way of trappin'.

When I got home, I showed my hand to a veterinarian there, and he told me I needed to go to the doctor and have him take care of it. If I hadn't listened to him, and just stayed home, everything would have been fine. But I didn't. I went off to see the doctor. They made a big deal about getting the animal there to check for rabies, but I knew I was alright. I was worried that they would take the animal, and I wouldn't get it back. I wanted the fur, so I skinned it, I just cut the head off and gave that to them. I had talked to Ben Bendrick about that, and he told me that they didn't need the whole animal; they just needed a part of the brain to test. He said, "You shot him? Where did you shoot him?"

"I shot him in the head."

"Well," he said, "Maybe there will be enough for them to check. But give them the head and see what happens with that." And it turned out that there was enough for them to use.

I had to go in every day for a shot. I got five shots. The guy at the doctor's office actually had to go to the drug store to get more of the vaccine. He was telling me that they were running short because there were many cases of rabies in the area. I looked at him and said, "Ya, I'm sure you do have a lot of rabies around here." I think they were doing that to make money because there were hardly any cases of rabies around that I ever heard about.

The Coyote and the Tire Iron

We were coming back from a movie in Wakefield on a winter night. Me, Louie Auchter, and his wife, Edna. We were driving down U.S. 2 toward Marenisco. The snow was pretty deep at that time. And we see this coyote come across the road. Something was pushing him, but I didn't know what. I could tell by the way he was moving that he was already a little tired. So, when he went over that big high snowbank, I said to Louie, "Stop! Stop the car! I want to catch that son of a gun!" Louie looked at me and laughed. I said, " I gotta have something to use as a club." So, Louie gave me a jack handle out of his trunk. I took it, and I went over the snowbank after him. There was an open field there, and the coyote was heading for this old log cabin that was there. It wasn't livable or nothing, it was just an old shack. And he was headin' for that. So, I widened out. And he stopped there by the shack. He backed his ass right up against the wall. Then I came in by him. Of course, I got the flashlight because I always carried that with me. And I got right up to him. I kept the light on him, and I had the tire iron raised over my head. I could see he was just ready to leap at me, so I swung the tire iron down and hit him right across the nose. I had to hit him again to kill him, but I got him and took him back to the car. Louie was laughing and said, "I have never seen anything like that in my life; you killing a coyote with a tire iron!"

Wolves

If I trapped a wolf and wanted to release him, the best way to do it, that I found was to get myself a stick about two feet long. I would hold it out there where he would bite it. He would hang on to that stick, and then I would back him up and tighten the 6 ft. chain where it was fastened, and push him back. So, he has ahold of the stick, and I got him stretched out like that, and then I could open the trap with my feet and release him. Sometimes they will let go of the stick right away, and sometimes they will hang onto it for a bit. I wouldn't let go of the stick until after he did, in case he wanted to get a hunk of me. I wanted to be the one with the stick. Wolves are pretty smart. He would be out of the trap, but still holding onto the stick. I knew if I let go, he could drop the stick and take a dive at me., So I needed to have something in my hand when they let go. When they did let go, they would take off, but not very fast. They would go a little way, and then stop and look at me. Then they would make some easy leaps. Again, not fast, a slight lope, a little lope, and be gone. Every wolf that I ever trapped acted that exact same way.

I kept a couple of them because they were small ones. There was a buyer who took one. He said, "Oh, this is a nice coyote..." I got top dollar for that wolf/coyote fur...ha ha." See, he had no problem taking the fur out of the U.S. into Canada. That was where he was from, and he had this big truck with all these furs, and the border people would just wave him through. After he got it across the border, then it was no longer a coyote; it was a wolf again, and he got big money for it. But down here, he had to call it just a "nice coyote." And I don't want any wolves around here either. There was a time when I took out quite a few.

CHAPTER FOURTEEN
Winegar Post 480

Chet Dumask is the last living charter member of Winegar Post 480, of the American Legion.

In 1946, with the return of WWII veterans and some WWI veterans, an American Legion post was trying to form. In April, 1947, Winegar Post 480 received its charter. In August, 1947, the Auxilary received their charter.

The town of Winegar quick- claimed the property, where the Vilas County Lumber Company Sawmill once stood, to the newly chartered Post for them to build a clubhouse. State Senator Alvin Okanski had a CCC barracks in his district that was to be torn down. It was offered to the Winegar Post at little cost, as long as the Post moved it here from the town of Alvin. The building was moved here and set up on blocks by Lassig Brothers, of Rhinelander.

The Post actually has two charters. In the 1950s, when the town changed its' name from Winegar to Presque Isle, the Post was also supposed to change its' name. But the Post members were opposed to the name change and re-chartered the Post as Winegar Post 480.

Chet explains:

"A bunch of us guys, Me, Richie Nemo, and a lot of the guys I grew up with around here worked on getting it going. Richie Nemo handled most of it. He got his father-in-law, Al Eschenbauch, to help with that. We ended up getting a building from White Sand lake, that had been used as a CCC camp.

We had to make a couple of different payments before it was paid for and got moved here. It cost us about $2,000 for it."

Since Chet is the last remaining charter member of the Legion Post, as a small tribute to him, the Ladies Auxillary, had a sign made to reserve a parking space in from of the Post. It says simply "Reserved for Chet Dumask."

In 2015, the Post members decided to create a memorial to the veterans of the town. It is incredible to me that this tiny American Legion Post, in this tiny town, under the committee leadership of Larry Gorrilla, somehow not only raised over $350,000, but used that to create a memorial that is one of the best in the state.

Allow me to relate a story of the groundbreaking for the memorial, and Chet's role in that event. Now, remember, Chet has lived there since the mid-1930s, and there is not anything that he has not been able to do in his time there. If he saw that something that needed to be done, he went out and would "Git R Done" to coin a phrase. The committee decided that Chet should be the one to fell the first tree on the memorial site, and he was happy to agree to do that. He was delayed in getting started though, due to the apparent strict adherence to the OSHA regulations about proper protective equipment. There they, all were, outfitting Chet in leather chaps, helmet, boots, gloves, safety glasses, and ear protection. Chet patiently allowed this process, even though he didn't really believe he needed any of those things.

To top it off, someone then asked Chet, who had been working in the woods his entire life, "Chet, do you need any help cutting down that tree?" Honestly, Chet could have probably cut down and trimmed ten trees in the time it took them to get him all geared up. But, he cut the tree down, and the site work was ready to begin.

The memorial was completed in 2017, and a dedication was held on October 14th of that year. This event was attended by over 600 people, and they were all thrilled at the sight of this beautiful tribute to our soldiers.

Preliminary plans are now underway to replace the main building, and once again, Larry Gorrilla, is spearheading that effort.

CHAPTER FIFTEEN
Forward

I hope that all of you have enjoyed looking back with me on the life of my amazing friend, Chet Dumask

As unbelievable as some of those stories may seem, they are, in fact, all true.

As I was doing my research for "Fearless", I realized something. When talking to people about this book early on, I would proudly proclaim that "I have known Chet Dumask since I was five years old". But I learned that was an untrue statement. In truth, I have known of Chet, since I was five, but I have only gotten to really know him since I started writing "Winegar Reflections", and now this new book, "Fearless".

I hope, as you have read this book, that you were able to ask yourself how you would have reacted to some of the experiences and situations that Chet found himself in over those many years.

- Would you have thought to break into the school, and make off with the teacher's piano wire to make rabbit snares, in order to feed your family?

- How would you have handled the task of retrieving the bodies of drowning victims, including the body of a young boy, and the body of a very dear friend? Would you have had the patience and drive necessary to have spent countless hours and days in the woods, just observing the habits of the animals that you planned to trap. Remember, that all of the tremendous success that Chet has achieved as a trapper, and outdoorsman, was because he taught himself.

- How many of you would have thought for a second that it might be possible to catch not one, but two live beaver at the same time, with your bare hands? As you have seen, Chet has done all of these things, and much more.

Certainly, over the course of his life, Chet has had some detractors, but those feelings mostly had their roots in jealously and envy. Some of the anger and resentment toward him was most likely the result of him besting them in either fights or feats. There are other trappers in the area that have achieved success over the years, but no one has the reputation and recognition of the "Best Trapper in the Northwoods", that Chet Dumask has.

It may seem somewhat odd to you that the final chapter is this book is titled "Forward", since that is usually something that is found in the very beginning of the book, and never at the end. There is a reason for this-

We have spent fourteen chapters traveling back in time, and learning about what I said in the Introduction—that this was a story of how a boy, and then a man was able to "survive and thrive, in the harsh environment of Wisconsin's North woods".

This book is coming to an end, but the story of Chet Dumask is still being played out. Chet turned 93 years young in April of this year, and he has told me that his goal is to live to be 100 years old. I don't think there is anyone out there, who knows Chet, that would bet against that.

Made in the USA
Monee, IL
12 July 2020

35652561R10090